YEMEN

*In the Land of the
Queen of Sheba*

GUIDE TO EVENTS

PALLAS ATHENE

Front Cover: Sana'a © Marco Livadiotti
Back Cover: Tribesman in Orange Turban © Marco Livadiotti
Title Page: Stele of a Woman with arm raised, 1st century BC, © British Museum

Picture Credits:
pp. front cover, back cover, pages: 4, 11, 12, 18, 26, 40, 49, 51, 52 © Marco Livadiotti
pp.1, 28, 29, 31, 32, 57, 58, 62, 64 © British Museum
pp. 8, 54-55 © Alexander Fyjis-Walker
p. 14 © John Shipman
p. 17 © Leila Ingrams
p. 21 © Wilfred Thesiger
pp. 23, 43, 61 © Martin Yeoman
pp. 25, 37, 38, 39, 44, 47 © Caroline Singer
p. 35 © Hugh Leach
p. 36 © Royal Geographical Society
p. 60 © Monica Fritz
p. 59 © Bader Ben Hirsi

Published by Pallas Athene 2002

If you would like further information about Pallas Athene books, please write to:
Pallas Athene (Publishers) Ltd., 59 Linden Gardens, London W2 4HJ
or visit us at WWW.PALLASATHENE.CO.UK

Publisher: Alexander Fyjis-Walker
Editor: Caroline Singer
Editorial assistants: Della Tsiftsopoulou and Ava Li
Translation and editorial support provided by Lisa Adams

ISBN 1 873429 95 9

Printed in the United Kingdom

Acknowledgements

Events General Co-ordinator: Marco Livadiotti

Yemen events organised with the participation of:
The Ministry of Culture, Yemen
The British Museum
The British Embassy, Sana'a
The Embassy of the Republic of Yemen, London
The British Council, Yemen
The General Organisation of Antiquities, Museums and Manuscripts, Yemen
The British-Yemeni Society
The Yemeni-British Friendship Association
The MBI Foundation
Special thanks to
HE Frances Guy
Husein Al-Amry
Adrian Chadwick
Stephen Day
Fadhl Al-Maghafi
Carolyn Perry
Caroline Singer
The Royal Netherlands Embassy, Yemen

Queen of Sheba: Treasures from Ancient Yemen
British Museum Exhibition
Sponsored by: Barclays PLC
Head of Exhibitions: Geoffrey House
Curator: St. John Simpson
Sheba Educational Events: Rowena Loverance and Nicholas Badcott
Solomon and Sheba, The Islamic Tradition: Venetia Porter
Yemeni Film Festival: Margaret O'Brien

Seminar for Arabian Studies
Sponsored by: The MBI Foundation
Organisers: Venetia Porter and Alice Bailey

Socotra Exhibition, Royal Botanic Garden Edinburgh
Sponsored by:
Republic of Yemen
The Royal Netherlands Embassy, Sana'a
With the kind participation of:
Anthony Miller and Ian Darwin Edwards, Royal Botanic Garden Edinburgh
Eduardo Zandri and the Socotra Biodiversity Project, Sana'a, Republic of Yemen

Freya Stark in South Arabia, Magdalen College Oxford
Sponsored by:
Abdul Aziz Ali Al-Qu'aiti
The British-Yemeni Society
Co-ordinated by: Caroline Singer and Hassan Abedin
With the kind participation of:
St. Antony's College, Oxford – Director of the Middle East Centre, Dr. Eugene Rogan
The Oxford Centre for Islamic Studies – Director, Dr. Farhan A. Nizami
Magdalen College, Oxford
Malise Ruthven
John Shipman
Hugh Leach
John Murray Publishers Ltd.

Yemen: In the Land of the Queen of Sheba
Guide to Events 2002-2003 booklet
Original concept: Marco Livadiotti

Sponsored by:
The British Embassy, Sana'a
The Foundation for the Protection of Antiquities and Cultural Heritage, Yemen
The British Council, Yemen
Editor: Caroline Singer
Publisher: Pallas Athene (Publishers) Ltd
Special thanks to:
HE Frances Guy
HE Mutahar Abdallah Al Saeede
Curtis Brown Ltd.
Stephen Day
Monica Fritz
Bader Ben Hirsi
Leila Ingrams
Hugh Leach
Julian Lush
Tim Mackintosh-Smith
Alexander Maitland
Anthony Miller
John Murray Publishers Ltd.
Carl Phillips
The Pitt-Rivers Museum
Venetia Porter
Malise Ruthven
Sarah Searight
John Shipman
St. John Simpson
Wilfred Thesiger
Martin Yeoman

Contents

Opposite: *Houses in Wadi Do'an*

The history of Yemen and its people stretches far back in time. This part of the Arabian peninsula was certainly among the first areas of the world to witness the dawn of human civilisation, and legend has it that one of the first rulers was a direct descendant of Noah. In the distant memories of many in Europe we remember the name the Romans gave the country, 'Arabia Felix', and wonder in these troubled times how travellers then considered this land to be 'Happy Arabia'. The wealth of the Sabaean kingdom that developed with the trade in incense and led to the vast irrigation schemes attached to the Marib dam, vanished with the rise of Christianity. But the stunning beauty of the landscape, the wealth of the country's history and the ever-present kindness and hospitality of the people are as true today as they ever were. The selection of articles in this booklet gives us a taste of the joys discovered by different travellers to Yemen in the recent past.

Those travellers included in this book have been an inspiration to many. Even today, the people of Hadhramaut talk proudly of their folk memories of Harold Ingrams, how he dressed and travelled like a Yemeni, and how he managed to implement the famous 'Ingrams Peace' which held together the tribal chiefs of the Aden Protectorate. Both Freya Stark and Wilfred Thesiger appeal to the internal longing in us all to find some harmony in our daily lives that transcends the mundane.

These are testaments to our shared history, as is the port of Aden, which occupies a special place in the annals of British history. From 1839 when Captain Haines of the Indian Navy captured Aden, up to the 1950s, the port continued to expand, until more than 6,000 ships stopped at Aden each year for refuelling, making it second only to New York in global importance.

Today there are tens of thousands of Britons of Yemeni descent living in the United Kingdom, and there are equal numbers of others who have spent many years of their lives in Aden. These ties are there to be built upon. I hope that the series of events listed in this booklet, which are due to take place over the next 12 months or so, will play their part in reminding the people of both Yemen and Britain of these historical ties – and help encourage new ones.

Through the unification of the two Yemens in May 1990, the Republic of Yemen today has been restored to a unity it has not seen since ancient times. Limited discoveries of oil have helped its people meet some of their economic needs, although more development is still required to bring all Yemenis out of poverty. But for the visitor, it is the magic of the desert palaces of Hadhramaut, and the stunning scenery as this side of the Red Sea squeezes the mountains together in a limited but breathtaking space, that will remain in the memory. Yemen is still a place for the more adventurous traveller but, as a privileged if temporary resident in this friendly country, I can assure those of you who are inspired by the tales in this book, that the adventure is well worth it.

HMA Frances Guy
British Ambassador to Yemen

It may be said that the multiplicity and diversity of cultures and civilisations constitutes the most vital and fertile source for fostering the continuity and further development of all human societies and their civilisations. Furthermore, different human experiences and the creative energies that emerge from them give life a more profound meaning, making it generally more enjoyable, more worth living.

Added to this is the fact that contacts established within the context of culture and civilisation open the way for meaningful and effective human interaction in other spheres of life, laying the foundations for a form of mutual understanding that is vital in the creation of solid trust and positive sentiments. Such contacts and interactions also form an important means by which to lay down roots for a higher level of harmony, which in itself enhances the common values and moralities that underline relations between societies and individuals, and give a more human content to the abstract concepts of virtue, decency and justice.

In this context, we sincerely hope that the important exhibition Queen of Sheba: Treasures from Ancient Yemen and all the related events taking place throughout the UK and in Sana'a during 2002-2003, will form an effective means by which to further strengthen and broaden the close ties of friendship and co-operation that exist between our two friendly countries, the Republic of Yemen and the United Kingdom.

The Yemeni civilisation, with its distinct local culture and Arab character, has made a significant contribution to the rich diversity that has spread throughout the Arab world, and into the wider world.

The exhibition can be seen as an effective way of developing invaluable contacts within a framework of different cultures and civilisations. The value of the Queen of Sheba exhibition is even greater because of the fact that it is taking place at the British Museum. This ancient and venerable institution attracts interest and profound respect throughout the world for its vital contribution as both a reference point for, and a trustee of, the cultural and artistic memory of human civilisation.

Having observed, albeit from a distance, the strenuous efforts of the organisers of the exhibition and the side events during the past few months, I would like to express my deep gratitude and appreciation to all involved in the realisation of this magnificent event.

Dr Muthar Abdullah Al Saeede
Ambassador of the Republic of Yemen to the Court of St James

The Cultural Foundation for the Protection of Antiquities and Cultural Heritage

The Foundation for the Protection of Antiquities and Cultural Heritage (FPACH) is a non-profit-making organisation established by a group of prominent Yemeni businessmen. It is the first of its kind to be established by the private sector in Yemen.

The aim of the Foundation is two-fold: to raise awareness of the wealth and significance of Yemen's cultural heritage, and to co-ordinate with local and international organisations interested in working to protect, restore and preserve the country's heritage.

Public awareness of the wealth of Yemen's heritage will be raised through media campaigns and by supporting a programme of high-profile cultural events and exhibitions both in Yemen and abroad.

The Foundation will act as a focal point for the identification and specification of cultural heritage projects in Yemen. This will involve identifying potential projects, commissioning detailed studies, presenting these projects to donor agencies interested in cultural heritage, and monitoring the work carried out by independent contractors.

For more information please contact:
The Foundation for the Protection of Antiquities and Cultural Heritage,
Sana'a Trade Centre,
Algeria Street, PO Box 12335,
Sana'a, Republic of Yemen
e-mail: heritage@y.net.ye

Opposie: *The cistern and houses at Thula*

Early Encounters – The First British Travellers to Yemen

Sarah Searight

British encounters with Yemen between the 17th and early 20th centuries began commercially, continued politically and only incidentally ventured into the cultural field.

In the 17th century the East India Company, desperate to find markets for English goods (the Indians were understandably none too keen on English woollens) decided to investigate the long-standing trade links between the west coast of India and south-west Arabia, through the principal ports of Aden and Mokha. In 1609, Captain Alexander Sharpie on his ship *Ascension* sailed into Ottoman-occupied Aden. The governor, a renegade Greek, was most unwelcoming and insisted on sending one of Sharpie's merchant companions, John Jourdain, under guard to the Pasha in Sana'a. This was not much fun for Jourdain, but it did provide posterity with a rare view of the city, the country and its government. Jourdain was reasonably well received by the Pasha, and was even allowed the honour of kissing his vest before hurrying back to rejoin the *Ascension*, now anchored off Mokha.

The next Englishman to visit Yemen came the following year under even more inauspicious circumstances. Sir Henry Middleton, another East India Company captain, was, like many of his seafaring colleagues, rather more pirate than upstanding merchant. He had already plundered Indian shipping at the entrance to the Red Sea, and perhaps not surprisingly, was jailed by the Ottoman authorities in Mokha when he refused to surrender his fleet. He was thrown into a dark and dirty dungeon where 'his companions were Grief of heart and a Multitude of Rats'. He eventually escaped by smuggling himself out in a barrel.

Rich pickings were indeed to be had around the entrance to the Red Sea at the Bab al-Mandab, and at one point the notorious pirate John Avery established a base on the island of Perim. It was an unattractive and waterless place, and his crew soon decided there was more to be made from the coffee trade at Mokha. The British had established a 'factory' (commercial base) there in 1618, exchanging British and Indian goods for coffee grown on inland mountain slopes and marketed in the Tihamah town of Bayt al-Fakih, some four days' journey from Mokha. Life in Mokha at the time was not easy. The authorities were unpredictable, the death toll from malaria was high and foreign merchants seldom ventured far inland. There were also long periods when the factory closed down, but luckily it was open when the German/Danish explorer Carsten Niebuhr and his ailing companions arrived in 1763, and the English merchants were able to offer them much-needed shelter.

In 1798, Napoleon's invasion of Egypt, which was intended as an assault on British communications with India, exposed the Red Sea as the strategic link with the Indian subcontinent. Shortly afterwards, this link was given even greater importance with the introduction of steamboats which plied the route between the Indian Ocean and the Mediterranean.

Steamboats required both well-surveyed coasts and coal, and it was the search for these, especially by Robert Haines who surveyed the south Arabian coast aboard HMS *Palinurus*, that led to some of the earliest discoveries of ancient south

Husn al-Ghurab or 'The Castle of Crows', and the ancient incense port of Qana

Arabian inscriptions. He copied inscriptions carved onto the dark volcanic cone of Husn al-Ghurab, the 'Castle of Crows', that scowls over the ancient port of Qana, west of Mukalla. Two energetic young naval officers, Lieutenants Cruttenden and Wellsted, together with the ship's surgeon Dr. Hulton, encouraged local bedu to lead them to other ancient sites such as Naqab al-Hajar in Wadi Mayfa'ah, a magnificent walled ruin dating from the mid- to late-1st millennium BC.

Not long afterwards, Haines took possession of Aden, heralding the beginning of a long relationship between this most splendid and ancient of ports, and the government of British India. The Indian Government had no desire to waste money on expanding British influence into the turbulent tribal hinterland, and adventurous residents were more likely to spend their energies exploring the Horn of Africa. But at the end of the century one man set out to explore the southern interior. G. Wyman Bury, alias Abdullah Mansur as he insisted on being known when dressed *à*

l'arabe, travelled indigo-smeared and suitably tanned, much to the distaste of the authorities in Aden. His account, *The Land of Uz* (republished in 1998), describes a world virtually untouched by European incursions.

The proximity of the Turks in northern Yemen posed a threat to the British in Aden – especially during World War I – which could only be countered by treaty arrangements with the hinterland tribes. This signalled the intrusion of outside politics and diplomacy, but it also led to some of the great cultural discoveries that we so relish today. 'The explorer must be a master of many arts, if the fatigue of his journey is to be worthwhile', wrote Lt. Col. Hamilton, the Master of Belhaven, an army officer whose travels, often in the line of duty, helped elucidate ancient south Arabian civilisation. His account, *The Kingdom of Melchior* (1949), is an object lesson in how to obliterate fatigue by focusing on the excitement of discovering such treasures as can currently be seen in the exhibition at the British Museum.

11

The Houses of Wadi Do'an

Freya Stark

Dame Freya Stark first travelled to Wadi Do'an in 1934, en route to Wadi Hadhramaut. She stayed for twelve days in the fortress-house of the Governor of Masna'a and his brother, who 'live together in harmony in the fortress, sharing the weight of government between them'. In this extract, she describes the mud-brick architecture of the region, and life within a Do'ani harem.

The good houses of Do'an are all more or less alike, their rooms supported on wooden pillars elaborately carved. The inner wall also is faced with carved wood, arched over the door and opening into niches where the store of quilts and pillows is kept by day. The carving is fine, and the old 'ilb wood is rich and dark: iron bosses, tinned over like dull silver, ornament it. The ceilings are built with strips of palm wood in a herring-bone pattern between small rafters; and supported on carved pillars with cornices flattened in the old Persian style; the windows are in four compartments, each carved in tracery over a small arched opening, for there is no glass at all; stout shutters, three inches thick to keep out bullets, close each compartment, and each window has a small round opening below it, with a gutter-pipe outside, useful to pour things on assailants below, and holes behind them for the barrel of a gun. For the valley has become quiet only in recent times, and many people remembered its little towns warring with one another, when the old Ba Surra was besieged in his own house, now so peaceful; and if a shot rang out, its echo beating from wall to wall of the wadi as if the sound could never escape that prison, the ladies of the harem would rush to their carved windows and look out over all the little towns spread in their sight along the valley sides, and wonder if it were beduin or soldiers, and then turn away rather disappointed when nothing further happened, telling me how wonderfully quiet the valley had become.

They took great pride in their rooms, and showed their riches by the number of brass trays which hung upon the walls, so thickly sometimes that they lapped one over the other: they can always be converted into cash because of the value of the metal, so that the ladies look upon them as a sort of savings bank, ready to their hand: the slave girls used to come and dust them with great care, though nothing else received the same attention, and they were always shining. Birmingham mirrors, odd plates, covered the rest of the wall space, and rows of tin coffee-pots, one above the other and almost touching, ran up the corners of the room to the ceiling. Otherwise there was no furniture, except now and then one of the beautiful carved chests, brass-studded, from Zanzibar, such as you also find in Kuwait and Basra. The floor of the room was covered with rugs, and underneath them the mud was hardened into smooth ridges like ribbed sand, a decorative wavy pattern also used on stairways. On the walls of stairs a frieze of mud was sometimes smoothed and whitened and worked over till it shone like distemper, with a zigzag edge to it: the cleverest workers of Do'an and Hadhramaut can use mud as delicately as

Opposite: *The village of Al-Hajarayn in Wadi Do'an*

13

stucco, and indeed nothing can be more dignified and decorative than the old fashion of their houses, which unfortunately, they begin to despise in favour of bad showy things from Europe.

Ahmad took me to see the building, where his masons sang to keep time together as they slapped the slabs of mud and straw into their mud foundation. Only the very lowest band of the house is laid in stone: the rest, even to seven stories high, is made of these slabs of mud and chopped straw, about 18 inches square and three thick, dried for a week in the sun, and then set in a paste of liquid mud. Donkeys were trotting up with water in goatskins to mix with the earth. The walls began to show: they incline slightly inwards like the old Sabaean buildings, and give their massive fortress look to the Hadhramaut cities; even the heaviest rain will not penetrate more than an inch or so into their thickness, and they stand for hundreds of years. Whitewash patterns decorate the outside of the windows or run

A Do'ani builder, photographed by Freya Stark

in bands alternate with the natural brown. When I said that I thought these houses more beautiful than the new cities of Europe, the two Ba Surras refused to believe me; but they admitted that perhaps their old carved doors were handsomer than the machine-moulded brown-varnished impostures just ordered from the West. The shades of civilisation are closing rapidly over these feudal valleys: only the absence of transport keeps our hygienic vulgarity at bay.

The first thing I asked for in my apartment was a bath, and a quiet time to struggle with the dustiness of my luggage. My room, like all these Hadhramaut apartments, had a bathroom of its own. An earthenware jar, four feet high, stood in the corner, filled with water every day: and the floor tilted down to a gutter which dropped the water over the face of the hill-side below our walls. The drainage, too, went down there in the same open manner, by a wide shaft on either side of which a small platform was built for standing on: and in the absence of toilet paper a niche was filled with clods of the hill-side earth, hardened in the sun. These bathrooms are clean and not unpleasant if they are well kept, and their disadvantages are felt only by the public in general if the area below happens to be a street. But nobody worries about that. When I was ill a few days later the ladies of Do'an assured me that my scented soap was the cause of the trouble; nor could I ever make them believe that their sewage might be more unhealthy than the perfumes of Houbigant, so anxious are people to think that what is good for one must also be unpleasant.

Ghaniya, my hostess, was simple enough. She had only a girl, and a boy called Nasir, whom she would look at with adoring melancholy and say: 'Unhappy one, he is an orphan,' so frequently that I felt sure it was developing a complex in him, for he was a morose and taciturn little creature, quite unlike the gay and talkative swarm of cousins all around him.

14

His sister was gay too; she used to come in with her little eyes dancing behind the two slits of her face-cloth and only looked serious if one talked about marriage, which was to be arranged for her in two years' time when she would be 15, the age for orphans, though ordinary brides can be younger. Whatever the age, the whole thing is settled without the child's knowledge: dresses are made 'for a cousin', and she only guesses what is happening when her hair is being washed for the event. Then her face is varnished yellow with *zabidbud*, a mixture of oil and wax and *hurd* (turmeric); her hands and feet are covered with a brown pattern; and she sits all through the third day of the wedding feast under a red veil which her husband lifts from her face at night. In the morning he leaves ten thalers on the pillow; and after the second night, a tray with a handkerchief, ten thalers, a pile of cloves, scent and incense; and after that, no more. We had one bride in the community during my stay: she was a bovine, good-natured creature called Fatima, still dressed in all her finery: she would wear it, she told me, for 40 days. Her black gown had a breastplate of solid silver plaited with cotton: her girdle jingled with silver tassels: her bare feet had anklets of gold. I covered her with confusion by asking her whether her husband kissed her, and if so where, for she seemed too highly decorated to be touched anywhere with any comfort. This indiscreet question caused her to be teased for days by her friends. Her mother, who stays with the bride for a fortnight after marriage, had just left.

The make-up of these ladies varied a good deal according to whether or not they had a husband to please at the moment. My poor Ghaniya divided her hair simply down the middle, 'because', she said, 'I am a widow'. Her mother also, who was a gay and delightful old lady from the next village, had long given up these laborious vanities and looked on the world and the gossip of her grandchildren with wrinkled and smiling detachment. But when Muhammad's wife came in, the lady of the castle, it was like a ship under sail, so rustling with bangles and girdle, so decorated with necklaces, and with so smiling an air of prosperity and favour. She was still a beautiful woman, though Nur, her daughter, had been married already for some years. Nur was my chief friend and companion in the harem, and used to bring my food and sit and talk to me, with one eye on the window for the valley and its doings below. She had the soft eyes, large mouth and long fingers of her uncles, and the same charming nature, an easy kindness to anyone who came: her husband had left her three years ago to work abroad, as most of the men of Hadhramaut do, and he used to write to her with every third or fourth ship that touched the coast. As it was the first time she had been left alone, she was allowed to come back and stay with her own people: the second time she would remain in her new home, for such is the custom of Do'an. The men stay away sometimes 15 or 20 years, and marry other wives abroad, since their own women will hardly ever leave their valleys. They go chiefly to Somaliland, Abyssinia or Egypt from Do'an, while the upper Hadhramaut emigrates eastwards to the Dutch Indies or Malaya.

Extracted from *The Southern Gates of Arabia*, John Murray, 1936. Reprinted by The Modern Library, 2001

Harold and Doreen Ingrams in Hadhramaut

Leila Ingrams

The name Hadhramaut occurs in Genesis as Hazarmeth, son of Joktan. Much of Hadhramaut's ancient history survives in legends, proverbs and poems handed down by word of mouth and in inscriptions found in ancient sites and along old caravan routes. The immensity of its barren plateaux and the awe-inspiring precipitous abysses transport you as you gaze upon this most primeval world. The territory itself takes its name from the mighty Wadi Hadhramaut, some 356 miles long, which lies far north of Mukalla, its coastal capital. The valley is renowned for its magnificent mud brick architecture, and has long been famous as a centre of religious learning. For generations, the region was bedevilled by blood feuds and tribal warfare, and by the scarcity of rainfall which made it difficult to scratch a living from agriculture. Many Hadhramis were forced to emigrate in order to support their families. They travelled to the Far East, India and east Africa to seek their living and sent home remittances. When they had saved enough, some returned to their beloved homeland.

It was to this ancient and fascinating land that my parents Harold and Doreen Ingrams were sent by the British Government in Aden in 1934, when Harold was appointed Political Officer. Within Hadhramaut there were two key areas. The Qu'aiti State of Shihr and Mukalla extended along the south coast and inland, while the Kathiri State formed an enclave in the north, with no outlet to the sea. The capital of the Qu'aiti State was the port of Mukalla, and it held several other important towns too, notably Shibam, famed as the 'skyscraper city'. The

Kathiri State had two key towns: Seiyun, its capital, and Tarim. At the time, the Sultans had only nominal control of the areas outside these towns, but both had a genuine concern for the development of their states, and an earnest desire for peace.

In spite of Harold being a colonial official, he and Doreen had quite uncolonial ideas, and were instantly absorbed by the world of Hadhramaut. They already spoke Arabic, and so were able to reach out to the people and explore the country. Outside their home they wore Arab dress, a custom which began when a prominent Sayyid (a descendent of the Prophet) named Abu Bakr Al Kaf, gave Harold a *futa* (men's sarong) and Fatima, his wife, asked Doreen if she too would wear local dress. The Qu'aiti Sultan also intimated to Harold, as a friend, that he might be more comfortable in Arab clothes, since my parents were the first Europeans to make their home in Hadhramaut, and in many cases they were the first Europeans the local people had ever seen.

Abu Bakr Al Kaf was a remarkable man. He strove for peace all over Hadhramaut and was a great philanthropist. Fatima was as kind and charming as her husband, and although she was not seen in public, my father wrote: 'men say to you confidentially "There's only one other person in Hadhramaut like Sayyid Abu Bakr, and that is his wife", because her influence spreads out unseen'. Fatima and Doreen would sit together talking of Hadhramaut and of their different lives. At times, Fatima would take Doreen's hands in hers and beg her to say 'There is no God but God and Mohammed is the Prophet of God', because she did not want Doreen to

Harold and Doreen Ingrams in Sei'ar country. The photographs were taken in November 1934 during their nine-week reconnaissance of the Hadhramaut region

go through fire to attain paradise, and she wanted to be sure of meeting her again.

A Peace Board was set up, and the first peace conference was held on January 24th 1937 in Seiyun. After warnings had been given to keep well away, punitive air action was launched by the RAF against the Bin Yemani tribe, because they would not pay the fine imposed on them for serious interference with road safety. As much as this bombing clearly disturbed Harold, it did have the effect of bringing in many other tribes to the peace talks. Travelling by donkey and camel, Sayyid Abu Bakr, Harold and others made journeys all over Hadhramaut to persuade the feuding clans to sign a three-year truce. Doreen, without Harold, travelled with Sayyids or beduins propagating peace, and had access to the women wherever she went. This was crucial for the women, some having lost husbands and sons in the fighting, and they urged Doreen to persuade their husbands (whom Doreen could also visit) to sign the truce. Altogether, some 1,400 signatures were obtained from the tribesmen, in what became known as 'Ingrams' Peace'. The Kathiri Sultan bestowed the title of 'Friend of Hadhramaut' on Harold. My father was greatly touched, since he

knew more than anyone how much Sayyid Abu Bakr had contributed towards the establishment of peace.

In 1952 Sir Michael Balcon, Chairman of Ealing Studios, decided to make a film called *Ingrams' Peace*, with Jack Hawkins playing Harold and Deborah Kerr as Doreen. Harold rejected the six master scene scripts, because Sir Michael hardly portrayed the Hadhramis and in particular Sayyid Abu Bakr. Nevertheless, a visit was made to Hadhramaut in 1953 to start filming, but Balcon soon realised he was defeated. He told Harold 'we will make the film when you're dead!'

After the declaration of peace came the surrender ceremonies. There was rejoicing in the streets, and women wept with joy. People felt secure to travel on roads and return to their fields to work. Trade began to flourish, the price of weapons slumped and it even rained heavily all over the parched country – 'a blessing from the Almighty as a reward for peace'. Later in 1937, the Qu'aiti and Kathiri Sultans signed a treaty with the Government of Aden agreeing to accept British advice 'in all matters except those concerning Mohammedan religion and customs'. Both stipulated that Harold should be the

The Hadhrami city of Seiyun was the capital of the Kathiri State during the Ingrams' time

adviser. The three-year truce, extended in 1940 for a further ten years, was enforced by the Hadhrami Beduin Legion which was begun by Harold and modelled on the Arab Legion of Transjordan founded by Glubb Pasha.

During this time, Harold was working on his classic book *Arabia and the Isles*. Sir Bernard Reilly, Governor of Aden 1937-40, wrote in the foreword to the book: 'in all his work, Ingrams has been encouraged and supported by the indefatigable collaboration and help of his wife. The name of Doreen Ingrams is as widely known as that of her husband.'

In April 1943, Doreen travelled with the first camel patrol of the Hadhrami Beduin Legion. They covered 530 miles in 29 days. 'The idea was that these beduins should be sure of a regular visit from government, so that friendly contacts would be made which would result in greater and better intelligence of what was happening among them.' Travelling in this way, Doreen witnessed the start of what was to become a disastrous famine. Many factors caused it: drought; the difficulty of importing grain during World War II; shortage of money with which to buy food when remittances from abroad came to an end, which resulted in the rich becoming poor and the poor unemployed. Harold and Doreen saw to it that food kitchens were set up. They started a 'hospital', and schools for beduin boys and girls, a 'children's village' for orphans of agricultural labourers, a school for the blind and one for the disabled. The RAF also played an important role, flying regular supplies of grain into the country. 'I had never imagined that such frail bodies could house so many worms, some a foot long, and often vomited from the mouth... it was the children who were most pathetic', recalled Doreen, 'their enormous eyes gazed round in pitiful bewilderment, and they died so quietly, one moment I would be cradling a child in my arms helping him to sip water, the next his little head drooped and he was dead... Anyone who has seen a famine-stricken country can never forget it.'

Harold's appointment came to an end and my parents left Hadhramaut in 1944, though they often returned for visits. 'Doreen and I had so identified ourselves with Hadhramaut and its people that we felt their country was our country and their people our people,' reflected Harold. Poems and stories were written and recited in memory of them, and people even named their children 'Grams' and 'Duree' in their honour. Their time in Arabia was to be the most significant period in their lives, for the Hadhramis and Hadhramaut held first place in their hearts. In Britain, they were invited to lecture to societies and institutions, and were awarded medals for their 'outstanding role in bringing peace to Hadhramaut', and for the contribution which 'their exploration of the region, separately and together, had made to geographical science'. Their publications were prolific and formed a unique contribution to the study of Hadhramaut.

In a postscript to *A Time in Arabia*, Doreen stresses: 'It is not just the policy we British followed as regards independence that I find regrettable in south Arabia, but also the fact that we did so little over a hundred years to educate and to involve the people in their own government. It is true that the Protectorate offered no return for the money invested in it and this was perhaps the reason, if a mercenary and inhuman one, to leave it alone, but in contrast the colony of Aden was necessary to us and we had built it up from almost nothing into a prosperous port...'

My parents had wanted so much to see Hadhramaut develop – that is what the Hadhramis wanted too. How happy they would be to know that there is now a university for both men and women. In 1996, Friends of Hadhramaut, a British-based charity, was formed to support educational and medical projects in Hadhramaut. Doreen was so pleased and moved to receive an invitation to be its first patron. On my own visits to Hadhramaut, I am often asked if Britain could do something more to help, given our long relationship and the Hadhramis' eagerness to learn English. Could we not build a school, a hospital? – for as the Hadhramis say: 'after marriage is gone, affinity still exists.'

In the Highlands of North Yemen

Wilfred Thesiger

Wilfred Thesiger visited Hadhramaut three times between 1946-48, the period of his two journeys across the Rub al-Khali (Empty Quarter), so vividly and poignantly described in his classic work Arabian Sands; *but it was not until 1966 that he first set foot in northern Yemen.*

During my years in the Desert, the Yemen had for me the fascination of hostile and forbidden territory, its tribes constantly at war with the Rashid and other tribes among whom I had lived. For years I had wanted to travel in that distinctive mountainous country in the south-west of Arabia. To the north the Yemen bordered on Saudi Arabia, to the south on the Aden Protectorate, and to the east, beyond the Jauf and the territories of the Dahm and Abida, it merged with the Empty Quarter. It was in this corner of Arabia that the true Arabs, the sons of Qahtan, were reputed to have originated, distinguished even today from northern Arabs, and it was here that the earliest Arabian civilisations, based on the incense trade, took root.

Thesiger was drawn to northern Yemen not only by its history and inaccessibility, but also by his experience of travelling along the Red Sea coast of the southern Hejaz in the mid-1940s. In June 1966, entering Yemen overland from the Saudi province of Jizan, Thesiger journeyed up the Qarra escarpment to the fortress town of Shahara on Jebel Ahnun.

Nowhere have I experienced more strenuous travelling than in the Yemen; we would scramble down thousands of feet into a narrow valley, labour up the far side, then down and up again across another gorge, with yet more beyond. Often in the evening I would see our next day's destination apparently only four or five miles away across the plateau, and yet it would take all day to reach it. The lower slopes of Jebel Ahnun were terraced for cultivation but only a single, narrow track gave access to the town of Shahara, placed like a coronet on the mountain-top. The massive houses, four and five storeys high, were built on the very edge of the precipice: from their windows the cliff dropped away for a thousand feet in a sheer fall. In the centre of the town a large cistern collected such rain as fell, and children bathed there throughout the day. Many houses had been damaged by bombing, yet so solidly built were they that sometimes half a house had been sliced off, but the rest was left inhabitable. Despite a haze which never lifted, the view from Shahara over this rock girt, treeless land was breathtaking, especially when the sun went down behind the mountains and the darkening chasms. And yet this view was not exceptional; during the coming months I was to see scores, all different, but all comparable in grandeur.

We descended the mountain and stayed in the magnificent castle of Qaflat al-Udhr. I had met some Udhr at Qarra and liked them. In the Yemen I was always on the move and never had the opportunity to know any particular tribe, but I would gladly have stayed a while with them at Qaflat al-Udhr. Their turbans and in some cases their clothes were dyed with indigo, which gave them a distinctive and arresting appearance, enhanced by the bandoliers with which they were draped and the large curved daggers they wore. Even young boys carried rifles. From Qaflat we went round the mountain to Suq al-Thuluth, the Tuesday market, where we spent an agreeable evening in a crowded caravanserai. Soon after dawn villagers started to arrive and unload their camels, mules and donkeys. At this market Royalist and Republican tribesmen haggled together round stone-built booths under two enormous fig trees. Despite the war, the everyday life of the countryside went on, and villagers could take their produce to market without fear of pillage. Yet almost every morning we saw aircraft and heard the sound of bombing, as we passed southward along the top of the escarpment.

Thesiger descended the escarpment from Mahabsha by a long steep track to Muharaq, and spent the next day at the crowded weekly market.

I was back in the Tihama, a world similar to the one I had known and enjoyed in the Hejaz 20 years before. The people, darker and quite distinct from the mountain Arabs, had refined gentle faces and easy, informal manners. Their clothes, too, were different: short white loincloths, tight-sleeved jackets, large straw hats and plaited conical skull-caps. They lived in wattle and daub huts. Each night they danced to the quick staccato beat of their drums.

Weeks later, travelling by a circuitous route via Kitaf and Najran, Thesiger made his way to eastern Yemen.

We spent a day in the Jauf among the Dahm. They had been our bitter enemies when I travelled with the Rashid in the Sands. Now I was happy to be among them, for they were bedu; even their voices reminded me of those bygone days. On a later occasion I stayed in their tents and there I met men who had known Musallim bin al-Kamam and who spoke of Bin Duailan, 'The Cat', who had died not far away in his last great fight against the Yam. 'Are you the Christian who travelled with the Rashid? Welcome! Hey, boy,

A young warrior, photographed by Thesiger

hurry and milk the red one. Hurry!' It was all so familiar; lawless as ever, the Dahm looted arms from Royalist convoys when chance offered, but I knew that while I was with them I was safe.

Yemen was still in the throes of civil war when Thesiger returned there in 1968, and his hopes of seeing Sana'a remained unfulfilled until his final visit to the country in 1977.

Yemeni labourers, working in Saudi Arabia, were now remitting to their families the equivalent of half a million pounds a day, and the disruptive effect of this undreamed wealth was everywhere apparent. The old walled city of Sana'a had so far escaped redevelopment, though in its narrow streets motorcycles had taken the place of donkeys, and television masts were on every building. Everything was changing fast.

Extracted from *Desert, Marsh and Mountain*, Harper Collins 1979, and in paperback 1995

21

A *Qat* Chew in Sana'a

Tim Mackintosh-Smith

In a house in the centre of Sana'a, I climbed the stairs to another room on a roof, grander than my own. On the way up, I called 'Allah, Allah,' to warn women of my presence. Panting from the ascent, I slipped off my shoes and entered the room. It was rectangular, with windows on all sides which began a foot above the floor. Above them were semicircular fan-lights of coloured glass. Into the tracery of the fanlights, and in the plaster of the walls and shelf-brackets, were worked the names of God and the Prophet, and verses of a pious nature – it was a very legible room. Polished brass gleamed everywhere: rose-water sprinklers, incense-burners, spittoons with little crocheted covers, the great cir-cular tray with its three water-pipes. Low mattresses covered with Afghan runners lined the walls. About a dozen men were sitting on them, leaning on armrests topped with little cloth-of-gold cushions.

I greeted the chewers, interrupting their *zabj*, the rapid banter, the swordplay of insults that starts all the best *qat* sessions. I'd scarcely sat down when an old man opposite turned on me.

'I was in Sa'wan this morning, and I saw this Jew. And, do you know, he looked just like you. You could have been twins!'

'But… but I haven't got any side-locks,' I parried feebly. Jewish Yemenis are required to advertise their religion by culti-vating a pair of long corkscrew ringlets.

'Ah,' he went on, 'you know what they say: "Jewishness is in the heart, not in the length of the side-locks."'

After half an hour of this verbal fencing, the *zabj* lost its momentum and devolved into solo joke telling. Yemenis, and partic-ularly San'anis, are a mixture of earth and polish, in contrast to their dour Saudi cousins of Najd and the unspeakably polite Levantine. Their contradictory nature was explained by the 10th century historian and geographer al-Hamdani as the result of the conjunction of Venus and Mars when Shem, son of Noah, founded their city: the Venusian aspects, he says, are 'religiosity, faithfulness, upright living, breadth of character, soundness in body, knowledge, poetry and dress, ease of living, and many other such qualities'; the influ-ence of Mars imparts 'a surfeit of passion, adultery, frivolity, fondness for music, singing and unseemly jokes, quarrelsome-ness, and a tendency to mess about with knives and allow themselves to be hen-pecked'. As for the women of Sana'a, while they are 'incomparably beautiful, swift and graceful', they are also 'prone to jealousy, coquettish and forward'.

Weightier matters are discussed at *qat* chews, and they are a major forum for the transaction of business and for religious and political debate. Many people also chew to aid concentration on study or work, and *qat* is the inevitable accompani-ment to all important occasions from weddings to funerals. A funeral chew is known as *mujabarah*, a word which also means 'the setting of broken bones'. But at the classic San'ani chew, it is 'lightness of blood' – charm, amiability – that is admired, not gravitas. At a *qat* chew, one walks what a 9th century poet called 'the sword-edge that separates the serious from the frivolous'.

My *qat* was good, a Hamdani from Tuzan. Qat is a dicotyledon known to science as *Catha edulis*. Unremarkable though it appears, chewers recognise a huge variety of types and are fascinated by its origin: when one buys *qat* one first establishes its pedigree. Quality is judged by region, by the district within a region, even by the field where the individual tree is grown and by the position of the leaf on it. The product of a tree planted inadvertently on a grave is to be avoided – it brings sorrow. *Qat* can be any colour from lettuce-green to bruise-purple. It comes long or short, bound into bundles or loose, packed in plastic, alfalfa or banana leaves. In Sana'a, as a rule of thumb, the longer the branch, the more prestigious it is: less image-conscious chewers – and I am one of them – buy *qatal*, the pickings from the lower branches.

A San'ani qat *chewer, by Martin Yeoman*

Just as in the West there are wine snobs, in Yemen there are *qat* snobs. I once found myself opposite one. Fastidiously, he broke the heads off his yard-long branches and wrapped them in a dampened towel. It was almost an act of consecration. When he had finished, he drew on his water-pipe and appraised my bag of *qatal* with a look that threatened to wither it. 'Everything', he said in an audible whisper, 'has pubic hair. *Qatal* is the pubic hair of *qat*. Besides, dogs cock their legs over it.' He tossed me one of the tips from inside his towel. It was as thick as asparagus, its leaves edged with a delicate russet, and it tasted nutty, with the patrician bitter-sweetness of an almond. There was a tactile pleasure too, like that of eating pomegranates – a slight resistance between the teeth followed by a burst of juice. I chased it with a slurp of water infused with the smoke of incense made from sandalwood, eagle-wood, mastic and cloves.

Qat does not alter your perception. It simply enhances it by rooting you in one place. There is a story in *The Arabian Nights* about a prince who sat and sat in his palace. Sentient from the waist up, his lower half had been turned to porphyry. 'I used to wish the Arabian Tales were true,' said Cardinal Newman. They usually are, to some extent.

After the *zabj* and the jokes, conversa-tions took place in smaller groups, then pairs, then, towards the end of the after-noon, ceased. I looked out of the windows at the city. 'There are three earthly paradises,' said the Prophet. 'Merv of Khurasan, Damascus of Syria and Sana'a of Yemen. And Sana'a is the paradise of these paradises.' Its mountains, says the historian al-Shamahi, are perfectly placed, 'neither so far away as to tire the eye when it focuses on the edge of the plain; nor so close as to stifle refreshing morning breezes or constrict the views that, just before sun-set, take on such wonderful colours.' They are mountains to be contemplated, like Fuji, if never so geometrical.

The climate, too, is perfect, if a bit dusty. And a little too cold in winter, added the traveller Ibn al-Mujawir, 'when ducks get frozen alive in ponds, with their heads sticking out of the ice. Foxes come and bite the heads off.' Very occasionally, it snows on the Prophet Shu'ayb [the tallest mountain in Yemen]. The event causes a certain linguistic complication, as Yemenis have no word for snow. You have to say, 'Ice that falls from the sky…No, not hail. The stuff that falls slowly and looks like cotton.'

Sana'a at street level is crowded and labyrinthine; but from this room on the roof you can see the green of gardens hiding behind walls of dun mud. The house façades themselves are never sombre, because of the plaster friezes that zigzag round each floor, increasing in complexity with every successive storey.

It is six o'clock, or five to twelve in the Islamic day that starts with the sunset prayer. But, for a time, it is neither: the Hour of Solomon has begun, *al-Sa'ah al-Sulaymaniyyah*. *Sa'ah* has among its root meanings in the dictionary 'to be lost, to procrastinate'. At the Hour of Solomon time refracts, as if bent by a prism.

No one speaks. Introspection has replaced conviviality. Somewhere, my fingers are working at the *qat*, polishing, plucking. When it was still light I found a fat horned caterpillar. A good sign – no DDT – but you don't want to chew one.

It is now quite dark. The coloured windows of neighbouring houses are lighting up, like Advent calendars.

We *qat* chewers, if we are to believe everything that is said about us, are at best profligates, at worst irretrievable sinners. We are in the thrall of 'the curse of Yemen' and 'the greatest corrupting influence on the country.' Yemenis themselves, while admitting that their habit is expensive, defend it on the grounds that it stimulates mental activity and concentration; they point out that at least the money spent on it remains within the national economy. *Qat* has also inspired a substantial body of literature, like this description of a handsome chewer by the 17th century poet Ibrahim al-Hindi:

Hearts melted at his slenderness. And as he
chewed, his mouth resembled
Pearls which have formed on carnelian
and, between them, an emerald, melting.

I can just make out my watch. Half past seven. Time, which had melted, is resolidifying. It is now that I sometimes wonder why I am sitting here in the dark with a huge green bolus in my cheek; why I and millions of others spend as much time buying and chewing *qat* as sleeping, and more money on it than on food. If we are to believe a major Western study of *qat*, we are 'making symbolic statements about the social order' and engaging in an activity that is 'individual, hierarchical, competitive'. Where you chew, and with whom, is certainly important. But to reduce it all to a neat theory – *rumino ergo sum* – is to over-simplify. It ignores the importance of the *qat* effect – something almost impossibly difficult to pin down, for it is as subtle and as hard to analyse as the alkaloids that cause it. It takes long practice to be able to recognise the effect consiously, and even then it sidesteps definition except in terms of metaphor, and by that untranslatable word, *kayf.*

Kayf – if you achieve it, and you will do if you choose the *qat* and the setting carefully – enables you to think, work and study. It enables you to be still. *Kayf* stretches the attention span, so that you can watch the same view for hours, the only change being the movement of the sun. A journey ceases to be motion through changing scenery – it is you who are stationary while the world is moved past, like a travelling-flat in an old film. Even if briefly, the chewer who reaches this *kayf* feels he is in the right place at the right time – at the pivot of a revolving pre-Copernican universe, the still point of the turning world.

In the room on the roof, sounds began to impinge: the rasp of a match; the noisy slurping of water; caged doves cooing; the snap of a twig to make a toothpick; someone buckling on his dagger. Then there was the click of the light switch. Everyone screwed up their eyes, blessed the Prophet, and went home.

Adapted by the author from *Yemen, Travels in Dictionary Land*, published by John Murray 1997 and in paperback 1999.

Opposite: San'ani houses. A qat chew will take place in a room at the very top of the house

Archaeology in Yemen

Carl Phillips

The pre-Islamic archaeological sites of Yemen display all the characteristics that archaeologists have traditionally used to define a civilisation. There are sites which would have been populated by urban communities requiring highly organised economic systems. Specialist artisans produced a variety of goods such as pottery and artefacts made of alabaster and other types of stone. These include simple containers, incense burners, offering tables, funeral stelae and statues. The ancient Yemenis also had the skills necessary to construct a wide range of buildings, from dams to monumental temples. One of the most significant features of the pre-Islamic societies of Yemen is its writing system, which was used by merchants, officials and rulers to administer economic and political power. However, although the archaeological remains of Yemen are very distinctive, and show strong locally-developed styles, it is clear that this was not an isolated civilisation but an important and integral part of the ancient world.

Surprisingly, despite all its attractions and prospects, not to mention the legends of the Queen of Sheba that surround it, the archaeology of Yemen has until recently received relatively little attention from professional archaeologists. It has chiefly been the epigraphers studying the ancient texts who have had the most available means to study Yemen's pre-Islamic past, thanks to a large body of south Arabian texts that has gradually been gathered by travellers, explorers and epigraphers since the early 19th century.

One of the most significant early advances in European awareness of south Arabia came from the discoveries made by members of the British ship HMS *Palinurus* which surveyed the southern coast of Arabia. In 1834-35 Lieutenant J. R. Wellsted visited two important sites, Husn al-Ghurab at Bir Ali, and Naqab al-Hajar in Wadi Mayfa'ah. He provided detailed descriptions, and copied examples of ancient Yemeni inscriptions at both sites. Wellsted is often acclaimed as the first to have discovered examples of ancient south Arabian inscriptions, but some of his colleagues from aboard the *Palinurus*, such as Carter, Cruttenden and Hulton, also published a number of inscriptions, and Wellsted was himself aware of others from north Yemen recorded by Ulrich Seetzen in 1810-11. Seetzen found inscriptions in the ancient Himyarite capital of Zafar south of Sana'a, and in 1811, shortly before he was assassinated, he sent copies of five inscriptions to Europe. However, it was the longer text from Husn al-Ghurab which enabled the German F. H. W. Gesenius to make the first credible decipherment of the ancient south Arabian language in 1841. Towards the end of the century, as an ever-increasing number of inscriptions was recorded, the values of all the signs of the alphabet were eventually established.

The first European to visit the Queen of Sheba's capital Marib and the earlier Sabaean city of Sirwah, was T. J. Arnaud, who produced a plan and description of Marib. He also visited the Awwam and Ba'ran temples and the Marib dam and its irrigation canals. In 1869-70, Joseph

Opposite: *Na'it, remains of the temple of the Sabaean deity Talab*

Halévy visited Yemen specifically to record pre-Islamic inscriptions. He travelled extensively throughout north Yemen and visited numerous sites including Marib, but unfortunately although he recorded the inscriptions, he does not seem to have made plans or illustrations of the other antiquities he saw. Between 1883 and 1892 the renowned orientalist Eduard Glaser made several journeys to Yemen and visited a number of sites between Aden and Sana'a including Zafar and Marib, where he surveyed the dam and provided important details about the Awwam temple. Glaser brought back a wide range of south Arabian antiquities which were lodged in museums throughout Europe.

Knowledge of south Arabia's inscriptions and ancient sites was significantly added to in 1928 when the first archaeological excavation was conducted at the site of al-Huqqa by C. Rathjens and H. von Wissman. At this site north of Sana'a, they excavated a Sabaean temple

A south Arabian bull's head in gold

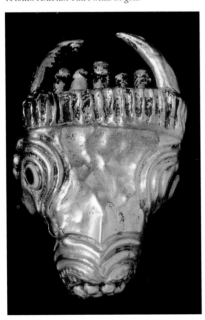

and studied other aspects of Sabaean culture including pottery, stone objects, metalwork and jewellery. Their discoveries soon captured the popular imagination, and their excavations received coverage in the *Illustrated London News* under the title 'In the Realm of the Queen of Sheba.'

Not long afterwards the first excavations were also conducted in south Yemen, at the site of Shabwa. More significant still was the excavation at Hureidha in Wadi 'Amd by Gertrude Caton-Thompson. Freya Stark accompanied the expedition and wrote an account of her experiences in *A Winter in Arabia*. Caton-Thompson was searching for evidence of the earliest human occupation in Hadhramaut, and found Palaeolithic remains at a number of locations. At Hureidha itself she excavated a small temple dedicated to the moon god Syn, and brought to light many aspects of the ancient culture of Hadhramaut. The results were published in 1944, the first report of a truly scientific excavation in Yemen.

The 1950s saw the arrival of the colourful expeditions of the American Foundation for the Study of Man, led by Wendell Phillips. He wrote a popular book about their adventures entitled *Qataban and Sheba*, but more important were the subsequent publications documenting the results of their work at the Awwam temple in Marib and the ancient Qatabanian capital of Timna. The excavations produced a wealth of material, and brought to light some of the most well-known archaeological finds from Yemen, such as the bronze statue of a warrior found in the enclosure of the Awwam temple, and the bronze statues of two lions mounted by infant riders, found in the ruins of a merchant's house in Timna.

The results of the American excavations at the site of Hajar bin Humeid near Timna were also very significant, and have had profound implications for our understanding of the development and dating of the south Arabian civilisation. From among the earliest occupation levels of the site, Phillips and his team recovered remains of ancient timbers which were radio-carbon dated to the end of the 2nd millennium BC. They also found a number of pot sherds from these early levels, with inscribed letters written in the south Arabian script. This implied that the alphabet was in use from the very early 1st millennium BC, and showed that Yemen's pre-Islamic civilisations were far older than had previously been thought. This early date was of course more in line with the probable dating of the Biblical story of the Queen of Sheba's visit to Solomon. While the excavations did not prove that the Queen of Sheba actually existed, it certainly established that Saba was an important and advanced trading nation from as early as the beginning of the 1st millennium BC.

The origin of Yemeni civilisation was – and to some extent still is – problematic. The 1940s saw evidence of Palaeolithic occupation in Hadhramaut, and Neolithic sites were discovered along the fringes of the Rub al-Khali, but there was no evidence from the intervening period of around 3,000 years with which to explain the development of the south Arabian civilisation. Scholars in the past have tended to explain it as the result of people arriving in Yemen from the Fertile Crescent in the north, bringing with them their advanced culture. However, such notions of mass diffusion and invasion are no longer in vogue with archaeologists. The roots of south Arabian civilisation are most likely to be found locally, in concert with the developments taking place in neighbouring regions such as the Fertile Crescent and areas of east Africa.

Excavations and surveys conducted since the mid-1970s up to the present day have now gone some way towards filling this 3,000-year gap and have revealed more about the early development of the pre-Islamic cultures of south Arabia. Participants from many countries, working

A bronze hand with a dedicatory inscription, 2nd-3rd century AD

with Yemeni colleagues and bringing together a wide range of disciplines, continue to unearth new information about the characteristics and evolution of Yemen's rich and varied heritage. This does not mean that Yemen's subsequent Islamic history is unimportant, or is not also being explored – it is. And this account of early archaeological exploration is unmistakably Euro-centric. One only has to think of the Yemeni historian al-Hamdani writing in the 10th century about the 'Antiquities of south Arabia' to realise that this is not just a European passion. Indeed, none of the important and exciting work being done today could be achieved without the active co-operation of our Yemeni colleagues.

29

Yemen, Solomon and Sheba

Venetia Porter

This small display in the John Addis Islamic Gallery echoes the exhibition *Queen of Sheba: Treasures from Ancient Yemen*. It tells the story of Solomon and Bilqis, the legendary Queen of Sheba, in its Islamic context, through a series of objects in the collection of the British Museum and the British Library. Solomon's role in magic and as Lord of the *Jinns* is explored, and Yemen's other queen, Arwa, known as 'the younger Bilqis', is highlighted. Also included in this display is another aspect of the cultural traditions of Yemen, with examples of the curved dagger known as the *janbiyyah*.

The story of the visit of the Queen of Sheba to Solomon is one of a number of stories that appears both in the Bible and the Qur'an. In chapter 27 of the Qur'an Solomon, while reviewing the birds, remarks on the absence of the hoopoe. The bird recounts on his return how he has travelled to Saba (the Sabaean kingdom of Yemen which flourished from the 7th century BC to the mid-3rd century AD): 'I found [there] a woman reigning over them, to whom everything has been given and who has a marvellous throne. I found her and her people worshipping the sun instead of God'. The hoopoe takes a letter to the Queen summoning her to Solomon. When she arrives, much to her surprise, her throne has been magically brought to Solomon's palace by the *jinn* and she is made to walk on glass-covered water. Once she realises Solomon's power she submits to God and becomes a Muslim. Her name is not given and to date she remains a mythical and romantic figure whose story is illustrated as much in

Western art as it is in Islamic art. It is not until the 9th century AD that she acquires the name 'Bilqis'. The story is elaborated in Arabic literature ever more fancifully and becomes a much-illustrated subject in Islamic art.

In Bal'ami's version, written in the 10th century AD, the writer expands on the account in the Qur'an. The mischievous *jinns*, fearing that Bilqis would monopolise Solomon's attentions, tell Solomon that the queen had hairy legs which is why they played the trick on her. The story then takes a strange turn: 'And Sulayman married Bilqis but he did not like the hair on her legs… so the *divs* made a bath of lime and arsenic which Bilqis stepped into and all the hair came away'.

In the Qur'an Solomon is described as a magnificent king, builder and metalworker. Not only were beasts, birds and *jinns* his subjects, but also the winds. The *jinns* worked for him 'making arches, images, basins as large as reservoirs and cauldrons fixed in their places'.

'And to Solomon We made the wind obedient: its morning course was a month's journey, and its evening course was a month's journey. And We made the fount of molten brass to flow for him. And of the *jinn*, some worked before him by the leave of his Lord; and if any of them turned aside from Our command, We made him taste the penalty of the blazing fire… Then when we decreed [Solomon's] death, nothing showed them his death except a little worm of the earth which kept slowly gnawing away at his staff…'.

Solomon's court with ranks of *jinns* and angels is wonderfully evoked on the lid of a 19th century Qajar goldsmith's box of

Solomon and the hoopoe (detail), goldsmith's box, Persian, 19th century

painted wood, while the phrase that begins his letter to the Queen of Sheba as recounted by the Queen to her courtiers, has often been inscribed. According to the Qur'an, the letter 'is from Solomon and it [says] "in the name of God the merciful the compassionate"'.

By virtue of his supernatural powers, Solomon is strongly associated with magic. His powers over the *jinn* were attributed to his talismanic ring on which was said to have been engraved 'the greatest name of God'. In magical texts and objects the 'greatest name of God' is represented by seven symbols. These include the five- or six-pointed star. The seven symbols altogether, or the star on its own, are variously known as 'Solomon's seal', and appear on a wide range of objects such as the backs of medieval bronze mirrors, magic bowls

intended to cure illness and so on, often combined with other magical symbols or Qur'anic phrases. A cast brass talismanic plaque has Solomon surrounded by his *jinns.* Around the edge are magical signs intended to resemble an ancient alphabet. Hieroglyphs and the Sabaean alphabets were considered magical in the Islamic period. Lines of indecipherable words and strings of letters are in the angular form of Arabic script, Kufic, which was favoured for inscribing amulets.

In the 11th and 12th centuries Yemen was governed by the Sulayhid dynasty who followed the Isma'ili Shi'a form of Islam practised by the Fatimids, their contemporaries in Egypt, and to whom they were nominally vassals. Queen Arwa, 'the younger Bilqis', ruled from about 1086 to 1138 from Dhu Jiblah in the highlands of

A janbiyyah *or ceremonial dagger presented to the governor of Aden in 1944 by the Emir of Dali'*

Yemen. Her court poet al-Husayn ibn 'Ali ibn al-Qam (d. 1138) wrote of her: 'If one were to adore, after God, a human being, then that human would be you and no other. And if your clothes were worn by Bilqis, then she too would not fear Solomon'.

The Sulayhids struck gold coins which closely resemble the coins of the Fatimids both in style and in the content of the inscriptions. Allegiance to the rulers of Egypt is shown by placing the Fatimid caliph's name on the Yemeni coins. They wrote the phrase 'Ali is the friend of God' in reference to Imam 'Ali, the first of the Shi'a imams, demonstrating their Shi'a association. Although Queen Arwa was running the Sulayhid state, she was not able to place her name on coins. Instead, they were issued in the name of her husband al-Mukarram Ahmad.

The curved dagger known as a *janbiyyah* is an important article of male dress in south Arabia, particularly in Yemen. Its use clearly goes back centuries and is attested in pre-Islamic times. A man's standing is judged on the basis of the splendour and value of his *janbiyyah* and the shape chosen depended on his position in society. The hilt is generally made of bone or horn, sometimes ivory. Rhinoceros was often used in the past until the trade was banned internationally. Coins, often imitation Venetian sequins, could be applied to the hilt. The blades are steel, the scabbards often elaborately worked silver. The *janbiyyah* is attached to a belt traditionally with leather thongs, although now this is more usually string and always bright green in colour.

Among the British Museum holdings is a *janbiyyah* presented to the governor of Aden Sir John Hall in 1944 by the Emir of the province of Dali', to mark a treaty of friendship with the British Government. The display also includes a number of loan items: an evocative drawing of 'a gentleman from Ta'izz' by Martin Yeoman; a *janbiyyah* with gold sovereigns on the hilt and a silver sword worn by the tribesmen of Yafi' lent by Stephen Day, and *janbiyyahs* and daggers lent by Leila Ingrams, whose parents, Harold and Doreen, were the first Europeans to live in Hadhramaut.

Freya Stark in Yemen

Malise Ruthven and Hugh Leach

Freya Stark first visited Yemen in 1934 at the age of 41. She wanted to explore the southern section of the ancient Incense Road, which stretched from the coast of south Arabia right up to the Mediterranean sea. Her main goal on this first trip was to reach Shabwa, capital of the Frankincense Kingdom, a fabled desert city of towering temples and unimaginable treasures which no westerner had ever set eyes upon. For Freya it was the ultimate challenge.

She arrived in Aden with influential connections, and stayed in luxury with the dynamic Frenchman Antonin Besse, founder of St. Antony's College Oxford and 'a Merchant in the style of the Arabian Nights or the Renaissance'. Besse's business empire extended from Somalia to Hadhramaut. He dealt in hides and coffee, frankincense and myrrh, machines, cars, radios, cigarettes and pharmaceuticals, and through his network of contacts and agents he smoothed Freya's passage through south Arabia. Later on, their relations cooled: Besse considered Freya insufficiently grateful for all his help.

From Aden she travelled by ship to Mukalla and spent a week at the Qu'aiti Sultan's guest house, gazing out onto the white houses piled under harsh red cliffs. She left 'with grateful feelings, and thought that, if ever I were to have a honeymoon, it would be pleasant to spend it on the curving beaches of Mukalla, where the rolling of the world is scarcely felt, with a small log boat to carry me and whomsoever it might be out all day among the porpoises and seagulls.'
Her journey up to Hadhramaut took her through the Jol. She spent six days and nights travelling across the parched limestone plateau with a party of bedu and their donkeys, sleeping under the stars and living off dried shark and small maize pancakes. Despite the hardship and monotony of the journey, Freya relished its rhythms and felt that 'when our human methods of transport are so perfect that physical laws no longer regulate our journeys by land or sea or air, why then we shall have outgrown our planet.'

Reaching the lush oasis of Wadi Do'an she spent several days cooped up in the harems of various mud-brick tower houses, sharing food with the women and listening to their stories. Unfortunately, she had arrived in the valley during an epidemic of the measles. She contracted a fever and spent a delirious week in the care of the ladies of the harem, who were convinced that her scented soap had brought on the illness. Although she rallied and travelled on to Hadhramaut, she never regained her strength and fell ill again in Shibam. She finally had to be airlifted back to Aden by an RAF bomber. Her book *The Southern Gates of Arabia*, which she rather sadly – and wrongly – describes as 'mostly a record of failure', is the account of this journey and her unsuccessful attempt to reach Shabwa. She was scarcely three days away from the ruined city, which through the unkindness of fate was to remain 'unattainable as the moon: I have trodden in dreams only the emptiness of its imperial road'.

Freya returned to Hadhramaut in the winter of 1937-8 with the formidable archaeologist Gertrude Caton-Thompson and the geologist Elinor Gardner, who were excavating the pre-Islamic moon temple at Hureidha. Freya's job was to handle relations with the local people, allowing the scientists to go about their business without interruptions. But almost immediately there were personality clashes, particularly between Freya and Gertrude Caton-Thompson, who she refers to in *A Winter in Arabia* as 'the Archaeologist'. Matters came to a head when Caton-Thompson pushed a labourer aside in order to examine a find, and caused a fight to break out. Freya perceived the archaeologist's approach to be arrogant and offensive to the local people. She felt that you cannot 'shoo these people away and still be welcome among them: the very corner-stone of their democracy is a general accessibility'.

When the expedition finally finished, Freya decided to travel on alone and explore more of the Incense Road. She made her way by camel south through the remote and secluded Wadi 'Amd, and through Wadi Shi'be, a narrow valley of scattered villages never previously visited by Europeans. After Naqab al-Hajar she joined a caravan of 27 camels down to the coast. She admired the way the bedus' few possessions were so much better adapted to this form of travel. 'One after one all my modern gadgets failed me; the thermos broke, the lunch basket was far too complicated... but the bedu's waterskin, with one hand used as a cup and a funnel, is economical and light; his coffee-pot, brass and unbreakable, hangs under the saddle over the camel's tail; his cotton shawl can be used for everything in the world that cloth is ever used for. He has all that is necessary and nothing superfluous.' Eventually the caravan reached the sea and headed east for Bir Ali, the site of the ancient frankincense port of Qana. Exhausted, Freya picked up a dhow and returned to the comforts of Aden.

When war broke out in 1939, Freya was back in Aden once more as an employee in the Ministry of Information. As a fluent Italian speaker who also knew Arabic, she was employed to counter Italian fascist propaganda. She travelled up to Sana'a which was then the capital of the Kingdom of Yemen, a place of medieval isolation ruled by an absolute monarch. Imam Yahya, who was both spiritual and secular ruler, looked to the Italians for assistance in his disputes with the Saudis and the British. But he also mistrusted them, and it was Freya's job to open up the gulf between the Imam and the Italians, and to try and further the British cause. On the grounds of propriety and diplomacy there was no question of her meeting the Imam face to face, and from her experiences in Hadhramaut Freya decided that the best approach lay through the harem. She held a series of tea parties for the leading ladies of Sana'a, including the wife of the Foreign Minister, and arranged for pro-British films to be screened. The newsreels of British fighter planes and ships made a tremendous impression, especially when Freya turned the sound up during the battle scenes. Eventually the Imam himself got to see the films, and when Italy entered the war on the side of Germany, Yemen remained neutral. Freya took a share of the credit and her career as an official propagandist began to take off. She was transferred to Cairo soon afterwards.

Freya Stark was not to return to Yemen for another 40 years. When she did so, at the age of 83, it was as the guest of Hugh Leach, then First Secretary at the British Embassy. He recalls some of his memories of her two final visits.

I first met Freya Stark in December 1975 when I called on her at her home in Asolo, northern Italy. She was in her early 80s, experiencing life's Indian summer while I, exactly half her age, was in the middle of my real one. When I told her my next posting was to Sana'a I sensed an acute interest, and the following March I received a telegram. It stated simply: 'Arriving Wednesday Freya'.

I had been warned that she could prove a demanding companion who might

Freya Stark in a village in the Tihama, during her final visit to Yemen

dictate our travelling agenda. The reality was the very reverse. She was invigorating, companionable, considerate, grateful and – at that advanced age – happy to be led rather than to lead.

On this first visit we located the houses in Sana'a where she had stayed 36 years previously, and unearthed a remnant of the Ottoman occupation in the form of a 78-year old Turkish bandmaster named Turmash Muhammad who, amazingly, remembered her. I can picture them now, conversing happily in Turkish together.

Travelling conditions in Yemen might have improved in the intervening years, but there were still plenty of unmade roads to jolt the bones of an 83 year old. One day she sat contentedly by the roadside for five hours, engaging passers-by in Arabic as we struggled to fix the gearbox of the Land Rover which had succumbed to the harsh conditions. We visited a number of high-land villages north of Sana'a and motored to Ta'izz for a three-day stay, entertained by local notables who were keen to meet her.

On her return to Italy she sent a letter stating that it had been 'one of the best holidays ever, and if you could put up with this elderly companion once more I should like to return'. This she did for three weeks in the following November 'to further improve my Arabic, it will make me feel young again'. To help her do this, I found a blind boy named Ahmed who sat and talked with her in my garden for two hours each morning.

During this second visit we made an extended tour of the coastal Tihama. She was in her element sleeping under the stars on the flat roofs of mud-built Tihama houses. She would often disappear into the women's quarters, and sounds of hilarity would soon emerge. Her visit coincided

Freya's great friend Sultan al-Qu'aiti of Shibam and family, taken by Lt. Col. Hon. M. Boscawen, 1929

with *'Eid al-Adha*, and we camped in the desert, cooked sheep over hot stones and hunted for hares. She asked only once for an extra day's rest, lying under a *ghaaf* tree whilst recovering from a stomach upset. She cured herself by her proven remedy of eating stodgy plain rice. She later recalled those days in a letter which describes 'the browsing flocks in the Tihama round our camps and all the stars wandering above our uplifted sleeping through the nights'.

I remember especially the long evenings together in my house. A glass of wine would draw her out, and she spoke of her life and loves, her conquests and disappointments. Though most would consider she had managed to squeeze at least three lives into one, she still felt unfulfilled and that, I think, is what drove her on to more adventures, more travel

and more writing.

Seeing her in action as a photographer I sensed that she had the inherited eye of an artist finding expression through the lens. Her camera, 'my little veteran' as she called it, was an early 1930s Leica III A, so favoured by travellers then and still used by myself. She was singular in her determination to take only black and white photographs.

We met subsequently in London a few times, and continued a correspondence for many years. When my memory dims it will be refreshed by her 30 or so letters. Her last read: '… a gloomy world dear, but sunrises and sunsets and much loveliness inside it.' I shall remember Freya as part of that loveliness, as will others who have travelled with her, or with the companionship of her words.

Socotra Island

Anthony Miller

The Socotra Archipelago is a small group of islands – ancient continental fragments – floating in the Indian Ocean off the Horn of Africa. Somalia lies only 80 kilometres to the west, but Yemen, some 300 kilometres to the north, governs the islands. To the ancients Socotra was famed as a source of precious gums and resins, including bitter aloes, frankincense and dragon's blood, which were prized throughout the Graeco-Roman world. Today the trade has gone, but Socotra remains famous – at least amongst botanists – for its bizarre plants and its extraordinary plant communities which remain almost perfectly preserved.

The archipelago contains four islands: Socotra, Abd al-Kuri, Samha and Darsa. Socotra is the largest, dominated by the towering granite pinnacles of the Haggeher Mountains which rise to over 1,500 metres in the north of the island. Their peaks are frequently shrouded in heavy cloud and mist, hence Socotra's ancient name, the 'Isle of Mists'. In total the archipelago is approximately half the size of the Canary Islands, but in contrast these islands are almost totally undeveloped, with only a fraction of the population – around 45,000 – compared with well over one million on the Canaries.

The people who live on Socotra are still largely reliant on their natural resources for survival. Apart from fish and some agriculture, they depend for most of their needs on wild plant products, and the introduced goats, cattle and sheep which 'harvest' the natural vegetation. In addition to providing food, clothing, shelter, fuel and tools, plants are also used in traditional medicine. For example, the bark of the dragon's blood tree (*Dracaena cinnabari*) is powdered and mixed with warm water to treat rashes and burns, while the tree's resin is smeared on the body as a cure for stomach pain and headaches. To protect such plants, strict rules have evolved over hundreds of years restricting the cutting of live shrubs and trees such as dragon's blood and frankincense, and controlling patterns of land use to prevent overgrazing. A delicate balance exists between the needs of the Socotran people on the one hand and the island's limited natural resources on the other.

Over 900 species of plant are to be

An early map of the Socotra Archipelago, Dutch, 17th century

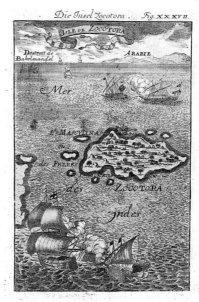

37

found on the archipelago, of which 300 are found nowhere else. This makes it floristically one of the richest groups of islands in the world. Even more importantly it is perhaps the only dry, tropical island group that is still untouched by modern development. As such it represents a unique genetic pool, and has been described as an Indian Ocean version of the Galapagos. It is home to several plants of potential economic value, such as the Socotran pomegranate (*Punica protopunica*), the only wild relative of the edible pomegranate. It is also home to several plants of horticultural importance including the Arabian violet (*Exacum affine*) and *Begonia socotrana*, one of the parents of all hybrid winter-flowering begonias and until recently thought to be extinct.

Even to the casual visitor the most striking thing about the island is the bizarre, often fantastic appearance of many of its plants. Trees with large swollen bottle stems and contorted branches dominate the lower slopes of the mountains, while a unique landscape of dragon's blood trees forms evergreen woodland on the upper slopes. From the top of their sturdy trunks spread a mass of regular swollen branches, each bearing a tuft of leaves which together form a rounded canopy. This tree has more in common with the Mediterranean flora of the Miocene period over 20 million years ago than it does with present-day plants. Its nearest relative is the dragon's blood tree of the Canary Islands, *Dracaena draco*, a relict species of the ancient flora which once stretched from the Canaries through the Mediterranean region to southern Russia. But while there are still tens of thousands of *Dracaena cinnabari* on Socotra, such is the impact of development on the Canaries that the number of *Dracaena draco* growing in the wild has dwindled to less than 200.

It is not only the plants that are rich in endemics. Probably over 90 per cent of the native species of land snails and 27 of the 30 species of reptile are endemic, while out of the 41 species of bird so far recorded breeding in the archipelago, six species (15 per cent) and 11 subspecies (27 per cent) are also endemic. These levels of endemism point to the ancient isolation of the islands from mainland faunas.

The key to Socotra's high endemism is its extreme climate and diverse topography – combining both limestone and granite mountains – which offer a remarkable range of habitats for speciation and survival. Endemics are found throughout the islands, even along the desertic coastal plains. It is the climate that is perhaps the most important factor; the islands come under the influence of both the south-west (Indian or summer) and the north-east (winter) monsoons. The south-west monsoon blows from June until September bringing hot, dry winds from Africa. During these months the island is effectively cut off from the outside world

A bottle tree in flower on the lower slopes

Dragon's blood trees grow on the upper slopes of the island

and life is very hard. The exposed plateaux and coastal plains are swept by fierce desiccating winds, while at higher elevations, and particularly areas facing the south-west, these same winds bring drizzle and cloud. Then from November until January, the winds swing around to the north-east and the islands come under the influence of the winter monsoon. These winds are lighter than those of the south-west monsoon and it is during this period that most rain falls.

The isolation of the islands and the strong traditional land-use management practices of the indigenous population have in the past protected the vegetation of the archipelago. However, with the building of a seaport and the development of the airport, Socotra is fast losing its isolation. An inevitable consequence of its opening up is likely to be a rapid increase in development activities and the potential breakdown of the traditional land-management practices that have in the past protected the islands' unique way of life and biodiversity.

Recently, two major conservation programmes have been addressing some these issues. The GEF/UNDP/UNOPS programme 'Conservation and Sustainable use of the Biodiversity of the Socotra Archipelago' focuses on community-based management of natural resources and builds on the successful traditional practices of livestock management. The British Government's Darwin Initiative Project 'Biodiversity Inventory of the Socotra Archipelago' is a collaboration between the Royal Botanic Garden Edinburgh and Birdlife International. Both programmes have been marked by a close collaboration between Yemeni and international scientists, and the people of the islands. Amongst the activities undertaken by the programmes are baseline socio-economic and biodiversity surveys, environmental education programmes and the development of a zoning plan for the islands. It is hoped that these will ensure the survival of this unique archipelago and its matchless natural history and cultural heritage for future generations.

Breaking New Ground: Film-making in Yemen

Bader Ben Hirsi

Making films about Yemen has been an unforgettable experience for many film-makers. Yemen is a magical country that stirs up a mixture of emotions. My first experience of film-making in Yemen was back in the early 1990s. Although I was amazed by the breathtaking scenery and the generosity of the Yemeni people, my first shock was that western film-makers seemed to be experiencing something else entirely.

Visually, there is no denying that Yemen is a mesmerising country with a rich and varied landscape. Filming scenery is never a problem, since one can point the camera at virtually any angle and still be spoilt for choice. But the Yemenis do have a different way of thinking and a different pace of life. This is not too outrageous if a director makes the effort to spend time understanding Yemen first before turning the camera on. Unfortunately this rarely happens, and film-makers are often eager to create an image of Yemen that they had conjured up long before ever setting foot in the country. One documentary stated,

Pier Paolo Pasolini in Sana'a during the filming of The Thousand and One Nights

for example, that the metal bars on the windows of stone houses in mountain-top villages were there to 'lock women in' and keep them from running away. How wrong can that be? Everyone knows that Yemen is a relatively hot country and when there are only wooden shutters and no glass, metal bars are a way of securing the safety of the children.

In another documentary, a female director walked into a village school to film a 'typical Yemeni classroom'. What she really wanted was a classroom full of boys, to show that there was no equality. When she arrived at the school with her crew, she was horrified to walk into a classroom full of happy chattering girls and only a handful of quiet boys. 'This just won't do', she said before speaking to the headmaster and insisting on sending out many of the girls and bringing more boys in from other classes.

One of the most powerful ways to shatter stereotypes and overcome misconceptions is through positive and accurate media coverage. This can only be achieved when 'facts' are true facts and the reporting of a country is based on time, effort and research. This rarely happens. A recent study of the depiction of Arabs in Hollywood revealed that almost 90 per cent of the images of Arabs and 'Arabia' cast them in a negative light. This is something that the Arab community must work together to correct.

My own company, Felix Films, focuses on projects that help create a positive awareness of the pan-Arab and Islamic world. From the number of Arab film-makers we have met at film festivals around the world, it is clear that there are many talented individuals with great vision and creativity. The main obstacle is the lack of pan-Arab organisations that

focus on funding Arab film-makers. Perhaps this will change in the near future: already, Prince Khalid Al Faisal of Saudi Arabia has pledged to set up a fund as part of the Arab Intellectual Foundation to help combat adverse publicity of the Arab and Islamic world in the West. But for now, the only option open to independent Arab film-makers is self-financed no/low budget film-making. A few European funds are available, but only as a top-up or co-production deal, and with this, an element of independence is lost due to rigid specifications.

Fortunately, the picture is not all gloomy. There are already many examples of films and documentaries which portray an enlightened image of Yemen, its traditions and its customs. A selection of the best of these are being screened at the British Museum as part of the Queen of Sheba season. Films to look out as well as my own, *The English Sheikh and the Yemeni Gentleman*, and *Socotra: Dragon's Blood Island*, include *Arabie Inderdite* by René Clement. This is one of the first films ever made in Yemen, and incorporates some amazing footage of life in Yemen from the late 1930s, and a rare glimpse of the Imam Yahya. Other films include the critically-acclaimed *The Thousand and One Nights* by Pier Paolo Pasolini which was filmed in many different locations in Yemen including Zabid. *Sur les Terasses de Rimbaud* by Saad Salman is also of interest, particularly since Rimbaud's own life was so fascinating. Caterina Borelli's film *Architecture of Mud* offers an interesting insight into the life and techniques of the Hadhrami architects and builders. It is very exciting to see so many good films on Yemen being screened during this exhibition, and it is an opportunity not to be missed.

An Artist's Response to Yemen

Martin Yeoman

When I first got to Yemen I wanted to draw all of it, everything. It was hard to focus at the beginning, because there was too much to see and take in all at once. I realised I would have to try and sketch what appeared in front of my eyes and take each opportunity as it came, rather than going out looking for certain scenarios or trying to capture whole streets full of people and buildings.

One place I decided to focus on was Bab al-Yaman. It made a powerful impact on me as soon as I saw it. I loved the fact that there was this magnificent gateway still standing, with a huge cannonball hole blasted through it. If it had been a National Trust monument the hole would probably have been filled in long ago, but instead it had just been left as it was, and I felt there was such a strong connection to the past. During my latest trip to Yemen I went to Bab al-Yaman every morning, and stood in the middle of the roundabout next to the metal fountain, with cars rushing past and the cassette shop behind me playing the same song over and over again. After a while people started to recognise me as the person who painted at Bab al-Yaman. They would call out to me on the streets – even in the really remote corners of old Sana'a I would be walking past and someone would call out 'Bab al-Yaman'. And a few people approached wanting me to draw them. One time a man came up and led me down a small alley to a carpet shop with an old man sitting inside. He asked me to draw him, so I did. When I had finished the sketch I showed it to the old man and he was genuinely amazed, he gasped. He didn't want to keep it though. He was happy enough to see that it really

was him on the page, and then he handed it back to me.

It wasn't always so easy, and I was conscious of having to tread carefully and avoid offending anyone, because not everyone likes to be drawn, especially in a Muslim country. One old man punched me in the chest as I was painting, for daring to recreate life. You also have to be selective. There are so many scenes passing you by every moment and you just have to let them go, but where you might lose out in some situations you gain in others. *Qat* chews provided the perfect opportunity to draw, because *qat* chewers sit very still for several hours. So I would have this wonderful row of faces and poses lined up in front of me, and I would listen to them talking about poetry and politics and God – because God comes into every conversation – and it was beautiful, a bit like being in ancient Greece I imagine, with this calm, reflective atmosphere in the room.

Some of the etchings that went into Tim Mackintosh-Smith's book *Yemen, Travels in Dictionary Land* were drawn on the spot. I had 36 or so zinc etching plates prepared with wax, and the idea was to use them like pieces of paper, drawing what I saw directly from life onto the plates with an etching needle. Having so many plates meant I could afford to relax, which has given the etchings more life and movement, I think. I also made drawings and converted them to etchings, and they had a different kind of life to them. I never intended to illustrate Tim's text directly, because we didn't want the pictures to be an artist's interpretation of a writer's words. I wanted to give my own version of Yemen.

The carpenters' souq, old Sana'a by Martin Yeoman

I liked working in old Sana'a, finding a little corner and just watching the world go by, seeing how people interact. There's something different every day, every moment. The old man who looks like he is dressed up as a pirate; the salesman selling plastic bags; the women covered in their *sitarahs* when the wind catches the material, so that suddenly they remind you of a Renaissance madonna with flowing robes. They are just tiny moments, but they encapsulate a lot.

People are much more used to foreigners wandering around now than when I first went to Yemen, but their friendliness has not diminished at all. I think one of my favourite memories was during my first visit back in 1987. I was perched low down on a piece of concrete, sketching a building. There was dust everywhere and a group of young boys gathered round to watch me draw. A girl approached, she was covered but I could tell she wanted to see what I was doing, so I lifted up my sketchbook and let her have a look. Eventually the kids got bored and left me alone. After a while, I noticed a figure out of the corner of my eye. It was the same girl. She came up and stood next to me, and a henna'd hand emerged out of the robe holding a big lemon yellow gobstopper. She handed it to me and then walked away. It was a beautiful moment, and so touching. I would love to go back to Yemen. It's unlike anywhere else in the world.

Arabia Felix, Land of Fragrance

Caroline Singer

In the ancient world, one country was believed to be favoured by Nature above all others. It was a land of abundant spices and aromatic trees, a place whose inhabitants were drowsy from the perfumes rising from their forests. This was a semi-mythical land; a realm where flying serpents and thick fogs swirled around frankincense groves, where the Phoenix rose from fragrant ashes with sticky resin on its talons, a country whose towns smelled like sacred altars and whose people cooked their food on fires made from the wood of incense trees.

Greek writers called this land 'Arabia Eudaimon'. In Latin it was known as 'Arabia Felix'. Both names translate as 'Arabia the Blessed'. Today, we call this country Yemen. It was 'the most southerly land of the inhabited world,' according to the historian Herodotus writing in the 5th century BC. The ancients believed that all the exotic, expensive resins they used in worship and medicine, the spices that added bite to their cooking and the incense that perfumed their houses and streets came from this wonderful place in the far south.

As with all myths, there were elements of truth to be found in the ancient stories. Yemen and neighbouring southern Oman were two of the only places on earth where frankincense and myrrh trees flourished. The spiny, twisted trees grew in scattered groves along the dry limestone wadis of the Hadhramaut region of Yemen and the Dhofar province of southern Oman. They grew wild and were impossible to cultivate. The perfumed resin that gathered in ducts below the surface of the bark was tapped by a handful of families who, in Pliny's words, were 'called sacred' because of the special rituals surrounding the process. During the harvest seasons, the frankincense-gatherers were 'not allowed to be polluted by ever meeting women or a funeral procession,' wrote Pliny. The resin oozed from cuts made in the bark, and when it had dried it was scraped into palm baskets and transported on the back of camels down to the coast.

It was here that the south Arabian frankincense and myrrh joined the spices of the east on a long overland journey to the temples, markets and streets of the Graeco-Roman, Babylonian and Egyptian worlds. Consignments of pepper, turmeric, cardamom and sandalwood from India, fragrant aloeswood from Cambodia, cinnamon and cloves from Sri Lanka and fine silks from China were sent in wooden dhows from the western shores of India, propelled by the monsoon trade winds to the southern edge of Arabia Felix, where they were stored together with the locally-produced luxuries. As well as frankincense and myrrh, Yemen and the neighbouring island of Socotra produced aloe plants, dragon's blood resin and indigo. In ports along the coast the precious spices, dyes, plants and resins were packed into leather sacks and palm baskets, tied securely onto camels and carried on an epic, parched journey over the mountains and sand dunes of Yemen, across the vast desert lands of Saudi Arabia and Jordan and up to the metropolises of the Mediterranean.

Opposite: *Frankincense is still sold in the souq of old Sana'a*

Great cities were built all along Arabia's trade routes, filled with marble temples and frescoed palaces and occupied by princes and merchants who grew rich on the taxes from passing incense caravans. Cities like Shabwa, Timna and Marib – the home of the Queen of Sheba – trading centres like Mecca and Medina, and the rose-pink city of Petra in Jordan all prospered from the proceeds of the aromatics trade. Today the ruins of Yemen's frankincense cities lie still and quiet, buried by desert sands. Only the husks of past civilisations remain, preserved in finely-carved limestone blocks and in the elegant curves of the ancient script.

The trade in aromatics reached its height during the 1st century BC, when three wise kings from the east were setting off on their journey to Bethlehem with gifts of gold, myrrh and frankincense. Legend has it that Balthazar, the Magus who brought frankincense, came from a small town in southern Yemen called 'Azzan. At this time, jars of frankincense and myrrh would have been considered superior to and more expensive than gold, for both were rare commodities, transported in relatively small quantities over vast distances from a remote land.

The law of supply and demand undoubtedly worked in the Yemeni merchants' favour. For at least seven centuries there was a huge market for their frankincense and myrrh throughout the civilised world. In ancient Egypt, myrrh was one of the main ingredients in the mummification process, while frankincense was heaped onto funeral pyres so that, as the *Egyptian Book of the Dead* proclaims, the soul can 'ascend on the smoke of the great censing'. In 1922 when the tomb of Tutankhamen was rediscovered, explorers detected a perceptible whiff of frankincense from the sealed flasks placed alongside the young Pharaoh. He had been buried over 3,000 years earlier. In ancient Greece, sackloads of incense were burned to honour Zeus, Aphrodite, Artemis and the other deities in their sacred shrines,

and placed on private altars to appease household spirits. The 6th century BC lyric poetess Sappho wrote in her *Hymn to Aphrodite*:

*Hither to me from Crete, to this holy
temple, where is your pleasant grove of
apple trees, and altars fragrant with
smoke of frankincense;
Therein cold water babbles through apple-
branches, and the place is all shadowy
with roses, and from the quivering leaves
comes slumber down.*

Further east it was the same story. If a Babylonian wanted to discover his future he would visit a libomancer, who gazed into the embers of burning frankincense and divined answers from the opalescent spirals of smoke. If he had a headache, the same man would make a small dough figure, pour water over it and prepare a burner of incense. As the water trickled away and the smoke rose, the headache would leave his body. And according to Herodotus, no Babylonian gentleman or lady would dream of making love without the accompaniment of fragrant woods and resins. 'When a Babylonian has had intercourse with his wife', he wrote, 'he sits over incense to fumigate himself, with his wife opposite doing the same, and at daybreak they both wash.'

Wealthy Romans in the Imperial Age cultivated perhaps the most extravagant craving for Yemen's aromatics. So we hear from Plutarch of the flamboyant vegetarian millionaire who treated his friends to a huge banquet with a life-sized statue of a bull moulded entirely in frankincense, myrrh and cinnamon which burned steadily throughout the meal; and of a rustic who tried to impress his guests by dressing asparagus in myrrh rather than in olive oil, which to his dismay resulted in an inedible dish. Arabian aromatics were burned to honour the Roman gods and to add ostentation to public games and private parties. The Emperor Nero is said to have ordered an entire annual harvest of frankincense to be burned at the funeral of his wife Poppaea – Pliny recorded details of the funeral with a disapproving tone, for in his view the price paid to the Arabian merchants for these luxuries was far too high. By the 3rd century AD Pliny's misgivings were proving correct: the Roman Empire was in decline, and could no longer afford to import eastern spices. Early Christians forbade the use of incense in church and the aromatics trade, starved of its most wealthy customers, sank into relative oblivion.

Today, only a few frankincense and myrrh trees still grow in Yemen, but the cost of a bag of frankincense or a pot of myrrh is within the reach of even the humblest of households. The air of the souq in the old city of Sana'a is filled with the scent of eastern spices: cinnamon bark and fennel seeds, thyme and tamarind, ginger, turmeric and peppercorns, cumin, cardamom, cloves and fenugreek, piled in sacks and baskets and weighed in hand-held scales together with henna and nuts, dried fruit and coffee husks. Frankincense is scooped from golden piles on stalls by the side of the road and poured into small paper cones, while myrrh is sold in dark, sticky lumps in shops crammed with glass bottles full of fragrances and essences from India. The smoke from these evocative scents perfume the streets and homes of Yemenis. They act as a potent reminder of the land the ancients once called 'Arabia Felix'.

Frankincense tree growing on the limestone typical of the Hadhramaut

How Coffee was Discovered

Once upon a time, high on a hill above the Yemeni coast of Arabia, lived a community of pious Muslims whose main source of income was a herd of goats that provided milk, meat and skins. One day a shepherd complained to the imam that his beasts were staying awake all night and leaping around. The imam reasoned that this strange behaviour might have something to do with the pasture, and he went to investigate the place where the goats had been grazing. There he found bushes with stiff shiny leaves and small hard berries with a large kernel. The imam cut off a branch laden with the fruit, and took it straight to a library in search of a treatise on botany. Alas, he could find no reference to the plant.

The imam noticed that the bushes all seemed to grow in straight lines, as if they had originally been sown by human hands. Who could have tilled the soil in that long-forgotten place he wondered? Legends told of a dark-skinned race from the Caffa region of Ethiopia who had settled in the lands of the ancient Yemeni kingdom of Saba and were ruled by a great queen named Bilqis. Perhaps, thought the imam, it was the Sabaeans who had brought this curious plant from their native land in Africa and planted it in Yemen.

In order to find out whether it was indeed the plants that were keeping the goats awake, the imam decided to try them. But they tasted horrible, and had no effect. Then he remembered that cereals were often toasted to make them more palatable, so he put some of the berries on the embers of his fire. They turned as brown as goat's dung, and produced an exquisite aroma.

He ground the roasted berries up into a liquid pulp and sweetened it with honey. Soon after drinking this dark brew, his heart began to beat so violently that he was forced to lie down. But instead of falling asleep he felt extraordinarily awake. His mind was rejuvenated and filled with wonderful thoughts. Soon his pious companions were drinking this new-found infusion, with the same miraculous results.

Yemen has a perfect climate for cultivating coffee. By the 17th century the Red Sea port of Mokha had become one of the busiest ports of its day. Ships would arrive from all over the world to load up with this precious cargo, and soon Dutch, French, Venetian and Egyptian merchants opened offices and consulates there in order to protect their trading interests. Within a few years, Yemeni coffee was being drunk in the drawing rooms and palaces of the richest cities in Europe.

In 1690 a Dutchman named van Hom transported a coffee plant to Batavia in Indonesia, and in 1727 the first coffee plant from Mokha was introduced to Brazil. The plants flourished in both areas, and the first ship-loads of coffee began to arrive in Europe from Brazil, Indonesia and later from Jamaica. The coffee grown in these colonial lands soon put an end to the monopoly held by Yemen. In the last two centuries, Yemen has continued to export its coffee in small quantities, and it is still considered to be one of the finest varieties on the market. The port of Mokha meanwhile, is now a small fishing village where only the ruins of elaborate palaces and fine mosques attest to its former splendour.

Opposite: *'Feast given by the Governor of Mokha', Charles Cochin, French, 18th century*

Tilius invenit.

Festin du Gouverneur de Mocka. N.º XVIII.

'The Most Beautiful Country in the World'

Marco Livadiotti

In 1970, Europe opened its eyes to Yemen thanks to the Italian film director Pier Paolo Pasolini. While shooting scenes for his *Decameron* in Eritrea, Pasolini decided to visit Yemen for a few days out of curiosity. It was love at first sight, and the visit prompted him to explore Yemen on many other occasions. Pasolini shot almost all of *The Thousand and One Nights* there, as well as scenes for the *Decameron* and *Oedipus Rex*. It was, however, a short film of just 15 minutes, shot hurriedly but with deep feeling, that sealed the love affair between the poet-film director and Yemen. Pasolini sent this film, entitled *The Walls of Sana'a*, to UNESCO. Here at last was someone who recognised the grave danger that threatened ancient Yemen. His brief documentary is an impassioned appeal for help: Yemen must be saved.

Pasolini would later say in an interview on the radio: 'Yemen is the most beautiful country in the world. Sana'a is a Venice built on sand.' He compared the cities of Yemen with Italian cities threatened with similar dangers. Yemen was one of the last countries to open its gates to the modern world, and it was this that now threatened to destroy an immense cultural and artistic heritage that had remained intact for centuries.

In 1983, UNESCO declared Sana'a a world heritage site, followed a few years later by Shibam in the Hadhramaut valley. In the 1990s it was the turn of Zabid, although this was unfortunately of little or no use, since today Zabid is gasping for breath, and the Dutch are attempting to salvage what little remains.

For millennia, Yemen has remained isolated from the rest of the world, as if by magic. Protected by mountains, sea and desert, Arabia Felix was a mysterious country to which few had access. The beauty of Yemen lies in its still being unspoilt. The fascination of its architecture is in its complete integration with the landscape. Everything is organised in terms of a perfect harmony between man and nature. Endless terraces, fortified hill-towns, villages and castles create spectacles in every corner of the country. Much of the land seems to have changed little since Biblical times; it is a country seemingly impervious to outside influence, in which invaders either adapted and mixed with the native people, or returned home. Thus the architecture is Yemeni, the landscape Yemeni, the traditions Yemeni. Yet this unique country is in danger of disappearing in the next few decades.

Saving Yemen would not cost much. It requires only a little common sense, less negligence and a few laws to allow the past, with all its treasures, to co-exist with the future. For years, world experts have come and gone at enormous cost but with meagre results. A site is protected, while its context is neglected or ignored. A city is saved, while ten others dissolve, creating a vacuum which can never be filled. Beautiful ancient cities like Dhamar, Ibb, Ta'izz, Mukalla, Amran and Rada' are now markets of cement and steel. The original urban fabric is forever destroyed and the historic centres are dismantled irreparably.

Yemen's architecture and landscape co-exist in total harmony: village in the northern highlands

Other ancient towns and villages with unique architecture such as Sa'da, Zabid, Seiyun, Jiblah and Kawkaban will soon suffer the same fate. The city of Sana'a is witnessing an unprecedented building and demographic boom that will soon lead to the sacrifice of entire quarters, some of which date back to the 6th and 7th centuries. Even today about 40 per cent of the original architecture of the city has already been lost.

Saving Yemen's heritage would benefit the whole of humanity. If the cultural and artistic legacy of this country disappears, the damage will be incalculable, especially for the Arab world. A serious policy of aid and protection from neighbouring countries is necessary, and moreover it is in their own interests.

The Yemenis are certainly aware of their predicament, and the government is trying to do something about it, but they need outside help. The whole country needs to be protected – not just isolated parts – by enforcing conservation orders and maintenance regulations, by proposing building and development criteria in keeping with the styles and traditions of each region. Restoration is important, but what is more crucial is saving the continuity. Otherwise the fractures between natural landscape and historic architecture on the one hand, and contemporary architecture and land development on the other, will deepen. Creating cultural, archaeological and environmental parks would allow the ancient rhythms of life to continue in harmony with the pace of modern life and new development models. Traditional building materials are still available at low cost. Restoring an old house costs less than building a new one out of cement.

In Sana'a, UNESCO has implemented a protection policy in collaboration with the local authorities, but unfortunately so far the results have been negligible. The mistake was to turn the ancient walled city of Sana'a into a world heritage site while neglecting the surrounding quarters, which are of equal interest, but are in a much worse condition. Today these quarters are rapidly disappearing and the old city is being strangled by new constructions that spring up at an alarming rate. Every day the old city loses something of its ancient aura.

Economically, Yemen's history could provide a secure investment, attracting culturally-minded western and Arab tourists willing to spend money in order to discover the country which, more than any other, has contributed to the development of Arab civilisation. It is still not too late to save Yemen's heritage.

Opposite: *The distinctive architecture of the area round Mahwit, northern Yemen*
Overleaf: *Sana'a and the surrounding mountains*

Yemen Events 2002-2003

*Dates, times and venues of Yemen-related events
in the UK and Sana'a during 2002 and 2003*

British Museum Events June – October 2002

www.britishmuseum.ac.uk

9 June-13 October
Queen of Sheba: Treasures from Ancient
Yemen
Hotung Exhibition Gallery, Room 35
Saturday-Wednesday 10.00-17.30
Thursday-Friday 10.00-20.30 (selected
galleries)
Tickets £7, conc. £3.50, under 11s free

Throughout the ages, the legendary Queen
of Sheba has evoked images of beauty,
power and wealth, yet she has remained
cloaked in mystery. This exhibition offers
an insight into the sources and interpretations of the Sheba myth, and uses
archaeological evidence from Yemen to
illustrate the unique character of the land
of Saba – or Sheba – from where she is said
to have come. The exhibition of over 300
objects includes visual interpretations of
the story of the Queen of Sheba's visit to
the court of Solomon, revealed through
Renaissance and later paintings, prints,
drawings and minor arts. These are drawn
from a variety of lenders, including the
Departments of Prints and Drawings,
Oriental Antiquities and Medieval and
Modern Europe at The British Museum;
the National Gallery; the Barber Institute
of Fine Arts, University of Birmingham;
the British Library; the Royal Scottish
Academy, Edinburgh; the Victoria and
Albert Museum, and private lenders.
   The rich culture of the land from which
Sheba came is conveyed by displays of
antiquities from Yemen, which reflect the
history, incense trade, daily life, religion
and attitudes to death in ancient southern

Arabia. The sense of richness will be further enhanced by music and the evocative
smell of frankincense. The objects themselves range from rare pre-Islamic gold
jewellery and incense burners to bronze
statues of the early kings of Saba, a unique
bronze altar and magnificent funerary
sculptures. Most of these antiquities have
been carefully selected from a travelling
exhibition organised by the General
Organisation of Antiquities, Museums and
Manuscripts (GOAMM) in Yemen, which
has been previously exhibited at the
Institut du Monde Arabe in Paris (1997)
and thereafter in venues across Europe
including the Kunsthistorisches Museum
in Vienna, the Staatlichen Museum in
Munich and the Palazzo Ruspoli
(Fondazione Memmo) in Rome. These
objects represent the highlights of the
Yemeni national collection, and it is a great
privilege to see them displayed in the UK
for the first time. In addition there are
important pieces loaned by the American
Foundation for the Study of Man
(Washington); the Ashmolean Museum,
Oxford; the Fitzwilliam Museum,
Cambridge; Cambridge University
Museum of Archaeology and Anthropo-
logy; the Royal Collections, Buckingham
Palace; private collectors, plus of course
some of the most important antiquities
from the Department of the Ancient Near
East at The British Museum itself.

St. John Simpson,
Department of Ancient Near East,
British Museum

A Persian manuscript of 1590, showing the Queen of Sheba and the hoopoe bird

April-October
Yemen, Solomon and Sheba: The Islamic Tradition
John Addis Islamic Gallery, Room 34
Saturday-Wednesday 10.00-17.30
Thursday-Friday 10.00-20.30, Free.

A small display in the John Addis Islamic Gallery in the British Museum telling the story of Solomon and Bilqis, the legendary Queen of Sheba, in its Islamic context, through a series of objects in the collection of the British Museum and the British Library.

June-October
British Museum Study Days
15 June, 10.00-16.30 – The Queen of Sheba
29 June, 10.00-16.30 – Archaeology and the Incense Route
21 September, 10.00-16.30 – Traditional Yemen
5 October, 10.00-17.00 – Red Sea Trade and Travel
All study days will be held in the BP Lecture Theatre. For more information contact the Box Office on: 020 7323 8181

29 June
Spice Quiz and Book Signing
Meet the author and enter the 'guess the spice' quiz to win a signed copy of Andrew Dalby's *Dangerous Tastes*, a history of spices and aromatics. From 13.00, in the Great Court. Free entry.

4 July
Dining with the Queen of Sheba
Enjoy a lecture, a Yemeni supper and a private view of the Queen of Sheba exhibition. From 7pm.
Tickets £49, Friends £45. Contact the Box Office: 020 7323 8181

26 July
Discover the Queen of Sheba
A behind-the-scenes day including a lecture by exhibition curator St. John Simpson, a guided walk through the exhibition, an object handling session, lunch, a drinks reception and a complimentary copy of the catalogue. From 10am. Tickets £100, Friends £90. Strictly limited to 30 people in two groups of 15.
Contact the Box Office: 020 7323 8181

August 2002
British Museum Family Events

This August, come to Sheba Summer at the British Museum and enjoy imaginative family activities accompanying the exhibition.
Arabian Mask Making – 5-9 August 11.00-12.30, 14.00-15.30. Ford Centre for Young Visitors. Adults with children aged 3+. £5 per child. Booking essential. Contact the Box Office: 020 7323 8181
Sheba Stories – 1-5 August; 8-12 August; 15-19 August. Performances at 11.00, 14.00, 16.00. Clore Education Centre, Free. Adults with children aged 5+
Yemeni Life Handling Sessions – 17-19 August; 22-24 August. 14.00-16.00. Clore Education Centre Adults with children aged 6+. £5 per child. Booking essential. Contact the Box Office: 020 7323 8181

British Museum Gallery Talks
18 June – The Queen of Sheba: Treasures from Ancient Yemen, Room 35
25 June - The Queen of Sheba: Treasures from Ancient Yemen, Room 35
3 July – Yemen, Solomon and Sheba: The Islamic Tradition, Room 34 (free)

A bronze head of a youth, 1st/2nd century AD

5 July - The Queen of Sheba: Treasures from Ancient Yemen, Room 35
9 July - The Queen of Sheba: Treasures from Ancient Yemen, Room 35
2 August – The Queen of Sheba in Western Art, Room 35
6 August - The Queen of Sheba: Treasures from Ancient Yemen, Room 35
9 August - The Queen of Sheba: Treasures from Ancient Yemen, Room 35
27 August – The Queen of Sheba in Western Art, Room 35
29 August - The Queen of Sheba: Treasures from Ancient Yemen, Room 35
3 September - The Queen of Sheba: Treasures from Ancient Yemen, Room 35
11 September – Yemen, Solomon and Sheba: The Islamic Tradition, Room 34 (free)
13 September - The Queen of Sheba: Treasures from Ancient Yemen, Room 35
26 September – The Queen of Sheba in Western Art, Room 35
2 October - The Queen of Sheba: Treasures from Ancient Yemen, Room 35
4 October - The Queen of Sheba: Treasures from Ancient Yemen, Room 35
8 October – The Queen of Sheba in Western Art, Room 35
9 October – Yemen, Solomon and Sheba: The Islamic Tradition, Room 34 (free)
All gallery talks start at 11.15am

18-20 July
Seminar for Arabian Studies
Supported by the MBI Foundation
The Seminar for Arabian Studies is an annual academic conference which has been running for over 30 years. It is the focus for scholarly presentations on all aspects of pre-modern Arabia. This year it is being held at the British Museum in the BP Lecture Theatre in conjunction with the exhibition *Queen of Sheba:Treasures from Ancient Yemen*. The three days of the conference will include papers by leading scholars on aspects of the history and archaeology of Oman and the Gulf, north and central Arabia, with a large component of the conference focused on pre-Islamic

and Islamic Yemen. The end of the conference is marked by a concert of Yemeni music on Saturday evening. £25 per day or £70 for the three days. Full-time students and British Museum Friends £8 per day or £20 for three days.
For further details, contact Alice Bailey on: seminararab@hotmail.com or Venetia Porter in the Department of Oriental Antiquities, fax: 020 7323 8561

Society for Arabian Studies Seminar Day 6 October 2002 at the British Museum. Contact sasbul@ijnet.demon.co.uk.

7 September
Yemeni Culture Workshop
A chance to examine ceramics, textiles and basketry from contemporary Yemen and explore their cultural and creative contexts. 11.00-13.00 Clore Education Centre. Tickets £10, Friends £8, conc. £6. Booking essential. Contact the Box Office: 020 7323 8181

2 September-13 October
Portraits from Yemen
Sat-Weds 10.00-17.30,
Thurs-Fri 10.00-20.30 (selected galleries)
Clore Education Centre
A display of recent photographs by Shelagh Weir, former curator in the British Museum's Department of Ethnography.

13-28 September
Yemeni Film Festival, British Museum

13 September
Solomon and Sheba
Director, King Vidor
1959, USA, 142 mins

14 September
Arabie Inderdite
Director, René Clement
1937, France, 49 mins
Music from the Heart of Yemen
Directors, Layih Abdulamir and Henri Lecomte
2000, France, 52 mins

A scene from Socotra: Dragon's Blood Island

20 September
The English Sheikh and the Yemeni Gentleman
Director, Bader Ben Hirsi
2000, UK, 75 mins
Socotra: Dragon's Blood Island
Director, Bader Ben Hirsi
2002, UK, 50 mins

26 September
The Queen of Sheba
Atlantic Productions
2002, UK, 50 mins

27 September
One Thousand and One Nights
Director, Pier Paolo Pasolini
1973/74, Italy, 129 mins
The Walls of Sana'a
Director, Pier Paolo Pasolini
1970/74, Italy, 13 mins

28 September
Architecture of Mud
Director, Caterina Borelli
1999, Spain, 51 mins
Hanging Gardens of Arabia
Director, André Singer
1990, UK, 60 mins

For more information and showing times, call Margaret O'Brien on: 020 7323 8896

Other events 2002-2003

1-15 June 2002
Yemen Outside In

An exhibition of photographs by Monica Fritz to be held in Sana'a.
Organised by the British Council, Sana'a.

New York-born photographer Monica Fritz's photographs have appeared in a variety of magazines in Europe and the United States since 1986. Now based in Istanbul, she has travelled to Yemen four times on assignments for English and Italian magazines. On her last visit, which was commissioned by the Aga Khan

Interior of a house in Shibam, photographed by Monica Fritz

Interior of a house in the Tihama, photographed by Monica Fritz

Architecture Award, she stayed for a year to work on a series of photographs for a book project. These photographs will be included in the exhibition to be held in Sana'a, entitled *Yemen Outside In*. The photographs show a variety of interiors as well as landscapes, cityscapes and portraits, taken across the country from the north to the south. There will also be a selection of her portraits of Yemenis living in Britain, taken as part of a British Council project. For more information contact The British Council: 00967 448355/6/7
www.britishcouncil.org/yemen

5 June 2002 onwards
Martin Yeoman - Yemeni Etchings
A display of Yemeni scenes by the award-winning artist
Abbott and Holder, 30 Museum Street, London WC1A 1LH
For more information call: 020 7637 3981

6 June – 6 October 2002
Freya Stark in South Arabia
Magdalen Auditorium, Magdalen College, Oxford

A small exhibition of black and white photographs taken in the 1930s by the traveller Freya Stark. The photographs are a selection taken from the archive at St. Antony's College, Oxford and document Freya Stark's travels in southern Yemen, from the coastal city of Mukalla up to Wadi Hadhramaut and back down to the tiny port of Bir Ali. Stark was one of the earliest European travellers in Hadhramaut, and her photographs evoke the mystery and beauty of its landscape and people. The exhibition also includes photographs taken in North Yemen on her last visit to the country in the 1970s.

Organised in conjunction with the Oxford Centre for Islamic Studies
For more information and for viewing times, contact Magdalen College Lodge on: 01865 276000

Etching of old Sana'a by Martin Yeoman

27-30 June 2002
Music Village
The Seiyun Group for Music and Popular Arts, a group of eight musicians and singers, will be participating in this year's Diaspora Music Village Festival. The music is a vibrant example of the cultural diversity within Hadhrami society.

27 June – Lunchtime concert at the October Gallery, 24 Old Gloucester Street, WC1. Free admission
28 June – Lunchtime concert at the British Museum for participating schools in the Music Village education programme
28 June – Evening concert for the Yemeni community at Goodenough College, Mecklenburgh Square, London WC1
29 and 30 June – Music Village open air festival at Kew Gardens. From 12.30 onwards. Free entry to gardens with Music Village leaflet

For details of all concerts and/or to obtain a leaflet contact the Music Village Festival Hotline: 020 7456 0404

9-13 July 2002
Arabic Arts Festival, Liverpool
This is the first festival of Arabic arts and culture to be held in Liverpool. It is being staged by the Liverpool Yemeni Arabic Club and the Bluecoat Arts Centre and aims to present the development of Yemeni community art within the wider Arab arts context. There will be a launch event on 11 July (1-3pm), a conference exploring the Middle Eastern image in the West, and seminars relating to Yemeni arts and community. On 13 July, the Yemeni musician Ayoub Tarish will close the festival, accompanied by Yemeni musicians from Sheffield.
A Festival Ticket priced £50 gains entry into all events and workshops. Advanced booking is recommended. For more information contact the Bluecoat Arts Centre on: 0151 709 5297

Inscribed bronze statue of an ass, 2nd century AD

17-21 July 2002
Yemeni Music
Three renowned musicians from Yemen, Dr Nizar Ghanem ('oud), Isam Khulaidi ('oud) and Jamal Aqlam (percussion) will be performing a series of concerts in the UK:
18 July – A talk followed by a performance at Goodenough College, London WC1
19 July – Yemeni Music night at the Kensington and Chelsea Town Hall, supported by the British-Yemeni Society and the Yemeni Community Association in London
20 July – Closing night of the Seminar for Arabian Studies, British Museum
21 July – A concert at the Town Hall, Sheffield
For more details, contact Fadhl Al-Maghafi the Yemen Embassy on: 020 7584 6607

5-12 October 2002
Middle East Association Trade Mission to Yemen
Targeting the energy, power, water, ports and industrial sectors. The first British trade delegation to Yemen for four years. Led by former Ambassador to Yemen, Vic Henderson.
For more information contact
Vic Henderson: 0239 226 5580
e-mail: henderson.vhi@virgin.net

July-August 2003
Socotra Exhibition, Edinburgh
An exhibition examining the unique biodiversity and flora and fauna of the Socotra Archipelago
At the Royal Botanic Garden Edinburgh.
For more information contact Anthony Miller: 0131 552 7171

Useful Addresses

For further information on the British Museum exhibition and the extensive programme of events taking place from June – September 2002, visit www.britishmuseum.ac.uk

For further information on all Yemeni events, visit www.queenofsheba.info

Yemen Embassy,
57 Cromwell Road,
London SW7 2ED
Tel: 020 7584 6607
Fax: 020 7589 3350

The British-Yemeni Society,
c/o The Hon. Secretary,
23 The Green,
Richmond, Surrey TW9 1LX
Tel/Fax: 020 8940 6101
Website: http://www.al-bab.com/bys/

Friends of Hadhramaut – a charity supporting medical and educational programmes in the Hadhramaut region. Contact: Friends of Hadhramaut, 48 Richmond Park Road, London SW14 8JT e-mail: hadhramaut @euphony.net

The Society for Arabian Studies,
c/o The British Academy,
10 Carlton House Terrace,
London SW1Y 5AH
e-mail: sasbul@ijnet.demon.co.uk

For further information on Bader Ben Hirsi's company Felix Films, visit:
www.felixfilms.co.uk

Yemeni Development Foundation,
Magnolia House,
73 Conybere Street,
Highgate, Birmingham B12 0YL
Att: Mr. Mohamed Al-Moassaibi
Tel: 0121 685 1800
Fax: 0121 685 1901

Muath Welfare Trust,
The Bordesley Centre,
Stratford Road,
Camphill,
Sparkbrook, Birmingham B11 1AR

Yemeni Community Association,
20-22 Craven Road, London W2

Yemeni Community Association,
167 Lodge Lane,
Liverpool L8 0QW

Yemeni Community Association,
71 Walford Road,
Sparkbrook, Birmingham B11 1NP

Yemeni Community Society,
34 Liverpool Road,
Eccles, Manchester M30 0WA

Yemeni Community Association,
Yemeni Community Centre,
Alice Street, Cardiff CF10 5BL

Yemeni Community Association,
18 Dolphin Street,
Newport, Gwent NP9 2AR

Yemeni Community Association,
35 Hatherland Road,
Eastwood, Rotherham S56 1RX

Yemeni Community Centre,
Highfield Lane,
Halesowen, West Midlands B63 4SG

Yemeni Community Association,
127B High Street,
West Bromwich B70 6NU

Yemeni Community Association,
9 Park Road North,
Middlesbrough TS1 3FL

Yemeni Community Association,
43 Attercliffe Common,
Sheffield S9 2AE

South Tyneside Yemeni Community Welfare Association,
19 New Green Street,
Southshields, Tyne and Wear NE33 5DL

Yemeni Islamic Centre,
50 Brunswick Street,
Southshields, Tyne and Wear NE33

Sheba Yemeni Charity,
18 Hinde House Lane,
Sheffield S4 8GX

Recent Books

A selection of some of the most recent books on Yemen

Aithie, Charles and Patricia, *Yemen, Jewel of Arabia*
Photographic book. Introduction by Mark Marshall CMG. Stacey International 2002

De Maigret, Alessandro, *Arabia Felix*
An exploration of the archaeological history of Yemen. Stacey International 2002

Dresch, Paul, *A History of Modern Yemen*
Academic, readable account of Yemen since 1900. Cambridge University Press 2000

Mackintosh-Smith, Tim, *Yemen, Travels in Dictionary Land*
Award-winning account of travels in Yemen. John Murray 1997

Searight, Sarah, *Yemen: Land and People*
Photographs by Jane Taylor, Socotra by Miranda Morris, foreword by Tim Mackintosh-Smith. Pallas Athene 2002

Stark, Freya, *The Southern Gates of Arabia*
Her classic account of travels along the ancient incense route. Published by John Murray, 1936, reprinted by The Modern Library, New York 2001

Thesiger, Wilfred, *Desert, Marsh and Mountain*
Thesiger's travels in Yemen and elsewhere. Harper Collins, 1979. Reprinted in paperback 1995

Wald, Peter, *Yemen, A Pallas Guide*
Up-to-date and comprehensive guidebook to Yemen. Pallas Athene 2002

Waterfield, Gordon, *Sultans of Aden*
The story of Captain Haines, Governor of Aden. Introduction by Stephen Day. Stacey International 2002

Simpson, St. John (ed), *Queen of Sheba: Treasures from Ancient Yemen*
Catalogue accompanying the British Museum exhibition. British Museum Press 2002

A bronze lion's head, 5th-4th century BC